Informal Classroom Observations On the Go

Feedback, Discussion, and Reflection

Third Edition

Sally J. Zepeda

EYE ON EDUCATION
6 DEPOT WAY WEST, SUITE 106
LARCHMONT, NY 10538
(914) 833–0551
(914) 833–0761 fax
www.eyeoneducation.com

Library of Congress Cataloging-in-Publication Data

Zepeda, Sally J., 1956-
  Informal classroom observations on the go: feedback, discussion, and reflection /
Sally J. Zepeda. -- 3rd ed.
    p. cm.
  Includes bibliographical references.
  ISBN 978-1-59667-196-6
  1. Observation (Educational method) 2. School principals--United States. 3. Teacher-
principal relationships--United States. 4. School supervision--United States. I. Title.
  LB1731.6.Z46 2011
  371.2'03--dc23   2011027536

Previous editions of this book were titled *The Instructional Leader's Guide to
Informal Classroom Observations.*

Sponsoring Editor: Robert Sickles
Production Editor: Lauren Beebe
Copyeditor: Lori Cavanaugh
Designer and Compositor: Rick Soldin
Cover Designer: Knoll Gilbert

Also Available from Eye On Education

Professional Development:
What Works (2nd Edition)
Sally J. Zepeda

Instructional Leadership for School Improvement
Sally J. Zepeda

The Principal As Instructional Leader
(2nd Edition)
Sally J. Zepeda

Instructional Supervision:
Applying Tools and Concepts (3rd Edition)
Sally J. Zepeda

The Call to Teacher Leadership
Sally J. Zepeda, R. Stewart Mayers, & Brad N. Benson

Classroom Walkthroughs to Improve Teaching and Learning
Donald Kachur, Judith A. Stout, & Claudia L. Edwards

Supervision Across the Content Areas
Sally J. Zepeda & R. Stewart Mayers

Instructional Leadership for School Improvement
Sally J. Zepeda

The Fearless School Leader:
Making the Right Decisions
Cynthia McCabe

Help Teachers Engage Students:
Action Tools for Administrators
Annette Brinkman, Gary Forlini, & Ellen Williams

Differentiation Is an *Expectation*:
A School Leader's Guide to Building a Culture of Differentiation
Kimberly Kappler Hewitt & Daniel K. Weckstein

Professional Learning Communities:
An Implementation Guide and Toolkit
Kathleen A. Foord & Jean M. Haar

On-the-Go Tools for Laptops

All tools discussed and displayed in this book are also available for free through Eye On Education's website as Adobe Acrobat files. Permission has been granted to purchasers of this book to download, save, and print these tools for classroom observations.

You can access the tools by visiting Eye On Education's website: www.eyeoneducation.com. From the home page, search the title of this book to find its product page. From the product page, click on the blue link near the top of the page titled "Log in to Access Supplemental Downloads." Enter your user name and password, or click on "Get an Account Now." On the next page, enter the following book-buyer access code:

ICO-7196-6

On the next page, click to download a zip file of the tools.

On-the-Go Tools for iPads

The informal classroom observation tools in this book have been configured for use on iPads. You will need to download a PDF viewing app to use these tools. Eye On Education recommends PDF Expert. With this app, you can view, complete, save, email, and print the 51 tools available in this book. You can also save multiple copies of the same tool for individual teachers and classes.

Please follow these instructions to get these tools on the go:

1. Using your iPad, search the App Store for "PDF Expert." (The full name of the app is "PDF Expert—Fill forms, annotate PDFs.") Install the app by tapping on the price button.

The next steps require Wi-Fi access.

2. Still using your iPad, go to the Eye On Education website (www.eyeoneducation .com) and find this book's product page by searching for the book title. From the product page, click on the blue link near the top of the page titled "Log in to Access Supplemental Downloads." Enter your user name and password, or click on "Get an Account Now." On the next page, enter the following book-buyer access code:

ICO-7196-6

3. On the next page, click to download a zip file of the tools. A grey screen will appear with two buttons. Click "Open in 'PDF Expert.'" Select "Okay" in the next window to save. The tools will now appear on the Documents page in PDF Expert.

4. To learn more about using PDF Expert and other ways to copy tools to your iPad, go to the Document page and open "PDF Expert Guide."

These directions are also available on this book's product page.
www.eyeoneducation.com

Contents

5 Talking with Teachers After Looking In

6 Studying Student Work During and After Classroom Observations

About the Author

Dr. Sally J. Zepeda, a former K–12 administrator and teacher, is a professor at the University of Georgia in the Department of Lifelong Education, Administration, and Policy and in the Program in Educational Administration and Policy. She teaches courses related to instructional supervision, professional development, and learning communities.

Sally has written numerous articles in such journals as the *Journal of Curriculum and Supervision*, the *Journal of Staff Development*, the *Journal of School Leadership*, the *High School Journal*, *NASSP Bulletin*, *Kappa Delta Pi Forum*, the *International Journal of Management*, the *National Journal of Urban Education and Practice*, *Review of Educational Research*, *International Journal of Educational Management*, and the *Rural Educator*.

Sally has also authored and coauthored 18 books, including the highly acclaimed second edition of *The Principal as Instructional Leader: A Handbook for Supervisors*, the second edition of *Instructional Supervision: Applying Tools and Concepts*, the second edition of *Professional Development: What Works*, and *Instructional Leadership for School Improvement* with Eye On Education.

She served for nine years as the book and audio review column editor for the *Journal of Staff Development*, and she served as chair of the American Educational Research Association Supervision SIG.

Sally is a member of the Council of Professors of Instructional Supervision (COPIS) and a lifetime Fellow in the Foundation for Excellence in Teaching. She also serves on the editorial boards for several scholarly and practitioner journals, including *the International Journal of Mentoring and Coaching in Education* and the *International Journal of Teacher Leadership*.

In 2005, Sally received the inaugural Master Professor Award from the University Council of Educational Administration. Sally received the 2010 Russell H. Yeany, Jr., Research Award that honors outstanding contributions to research, and in 2011, she received the Distinguished Research Mentor Award from the University of Georgia.

As a professor-in-residence with the Clarke County School District (Athens, GA), Sally is assisting with the rollout of a teacher evaluation system and providing professional development for school leaders as they work with teachers to improve student learning.

Introduction
to the Third Edition

Several opportunities and challenges presented themselves when I began planning the third edition of *The Instructional Leader's Guide to Informal Classroom Observations.* I recognized that there was a need to purposefully acknowledge the shift in who conducts classroom observations. Like other administrative tasks that in the past were conducted almost exclusively by principals, informal classroom observations are an essential work function and are now being conducted by a host of other educators, such as Teacher Specialists, Learning Support Specialists, Reading and Math Coaches, School Improvement Coaches, Content Coordinators, Teacher Leaders, High School Department Chairs, etc. One of the most significant revisions of this book is that it has been expanded to recognize the influential roles of other educators who spend time working in classrooms with teachers and their students. I also felt a need to change the title of the third edition to reflect that the book can be used by those individuals who do not necessarily see themselves as "instructional leaders."

In addition to the reproducible tools available in the back of the book, this edition also includes a Tool Index (page 183) to assist with planning and organizing classroom observations.

Another significant change in the new edition is the acknowledgement of the expanding presence of technology in today's schools. The tools[1] in this book have been created for the busy, on-the-go observer who needs thorough and efficient tools to record classroom observations and aid meaningful feedback in postobservation conferences. It is difficult to imagine how technologically unsophisticated our schools were when the first edition of this book was released back in 2005. As in previous editions, observers can still conduct their observations using pencil and paper tools. In the new edition, you can use the observation tools on your laptop computer, iPad, or other electronic device. For more information, visit this book's product page at www.eyeoneducation.com.

Since the publication of the first edition, schools have become more systematic about the way they look at teacher performance and have adopted standards and benchmarks, one of the most popular being Charlotte Danielson's *Enhancing Professional Practice: A Framework for Teaching* (1996, 2007). Like the *Framework*, this book is designed to support professional development and improve teacher skills. Organized into four domains (Planning and Preparation, Classroom Environment, Instruction, and Professional Responsibilities), the *Framework* components can be used along with the observation

---

[1] Throughout this book, credit is given to the practitioners who created some of the tools presented here. For the purposes of this third edition, I kept the titles and affiliations held by these practitioners at the time the tools were created.

tools in this book. This is important because the ability to make meaningful classroom observations is necessary to promote effective teaching. In addition, the tools in this book can be used in tandem with any system that promotes teacher growth and development.

I invite you to examine the tools in detail as they encompass the many elements of what we expect for effective teaching, an orderly classroom, the differentiation of instruction, the use of cooperative learning, the start and/or end of the class period, the use of questioning skills, and the assessment of learning, to name a few. The classroom observation tools are designed to enable the classroom observer to develop a focus within the first minute or so of entering the room. With a focus set at the onset of the observation, the classroom observer can use the tools to start recording the events of the classroom. The tools can guide the observer in efficiently and thoroughly recording information about what he or she sees as teachers and students interact, how they work through content, how the standards of instruction unfold, what he or she hears students and teachers talk about during the lesson, and how students and teachers actively assess learning. These tools also promote valuable discussion in feedback conferences.

For teachers, informal classroom observations support continuous professional growth. Appropriate tools that capture the events of the classroom are needed to conduct meaningful informal classroom observations. By monitoring instruction through the use of the tools in this book, both the observer and the teacher can have more focused feedback conferences and identify areas for improvement.

For administrators, it is important to use teacher evaluation systems that include both formal and informal classroom observations. This book can assist in conducting informal classroom observations that complement the more formal observations associated with annual review processes. The tools found in this book are designed to help administrators give effective feedback to improve instruction and student learning.

The tools are powerful because, when adapted to fit the context of a school and its classrooms, a more comprehensive examination and analysis of instructional practices and student learning can occur between the teacher and the observer.

Top 10 Tools

Although the 51 informal classroom observation tools in this book have been designed uniquely with different methods and approaches to suit individual needs, I recognize that today's educators are busy people and may not have the time to read this book cover to cover. Therefore, I offer my selection of the top 10 tools that educators in the field of practice have found helpful.

I invite you to share your own top 10 picks with me as you use the tools to help conduct informal classroom observations.

Sally J. Zepeda

1
Readying for Informal Classroom Observations

In This Chapter...
♦ Informal classroom observations are important.
♦ Supervisors and coaches make the commitment to get out and about.
♦ Supervisors and coaches know their people.
♦ Leaders assess the context of supervision and their own beliefs.
♦ Principals develop the leadership skills of the administrative team.
♦ Supervisors and coaches develop practices to track observation efforts.

This chapter includes tools designed to help supervisors and coaches emerge as leaders while conducting informal classroom observations. The following tools are offered:

A resounding finding in the literature of the accountability movement is that teacher quality improves student learning. Additionally, supervision of instruction is integral to district-wide plans for reform (Palandra, 2010). If this premise is true, then the assessment of teaching in classrooms needs to become the first step toward improving instruction and assisting teachers to examine their practices. Assisting teachers begins at the place where instruction occurs: the classroom. Principals are no longer the only school personnel who are concerned with teacher quality. One way to support teacher learning and growth is to engage teachers in examining their own practices through informal classroom observations. There are many people whose titles range from principal to assistant principal, from high school department chair to grade level leader, and from teacher leader to central office leader who conduct informal classroom observations. Often, anyone who conducts classroom observations is referred to as a leader, regardless of title or position within the school system. This book supports anyone who engages in informal classroom observations. Remember, like students, teachers need opportunities to grow, develop, and learn. One of the ways to promote teacher learning and improvement is an informal classroom observation. People who conduct classroom observations are commonly referred to as supervisors or coaches. In this book, we use the terms *supervisor* and *coach* to denote any school personnel conducting informal classroom observations with teachers.

What Is This Book About?

This book focuses on assisting supervisors and coaches as they work with teachers in formative ways, primarily through informal classroom observations. To make informal classroom observations a priority, supervisors and coaches must frame their work habits and daily routines around dropping by classrooms and then following up by providing teachers with feedback and opportunities for reflection and inquiry. This book was written for supervisors and coaches who want to be viewed by teachers as a support for instructional programs. Assistant principals, department chairs, lead teachers, teacher leaders, and others can enhance the instructional program by developing a better understanding of informal classroom observations that support teacher development and growth.

This book provides a series of classroom observation tools to help frame informal classroom observation and follow-up discussions with teachers. This third edition includes additional classroom observation tools that have been field-tested by school personnel. There is also an updated chapter with tips and cues on how to incorporate examining student work and other artifacts in postobservation conversations.

Supervisors and coaches are encouraged to use and adapt the tools in this book. The value of the tools and techniques offered is that they are easily adaptable. Principals, assistant principals, supervisors, coaches, and teacher leaders do not need to use every tool to be effective instructional leaders. Pick the tools that make sense and use existing tools to develop even more tools to meet the needs of teachers in your school. These tools are available to you in three different ways. In each chapter, you'll see how the tools can be implemented by an instructional leader during classroom observations, as well as in postobservation conferences. In the "Reproducible Classroom Observation Tools" section (page 127), you will find blank versions of the same tools that appear throughout the book. Permission is granted to those who have purchased this book to photocopy blank forms and use them while working with teachers. Blank versions of the tools can also be downloaded from Eye On Education's Web site: www.eyeoneducation.com. (See page v for details.)

Why Informal Classroom Observations Are Important

The informal classroom observation is a way to get instructional supervision and teacher evaluation out of the main office. Teachers need feedback more than once or twice a school year. Teachers need formative feedback, not just summative. Informal classroom observations provide valuable opportunities for more frequent interaction between the supervisor and the teacher in a nonthreatening, nonevaluative manner. Informal classroom observations can provide opportunities to extend the talk about teaching, if the supervisor and coach carve out enough time after the observation to engage teachers in a discussion about their instructional practices during the postobservation conferences.

Recently, informal classroom observations have become vogue with principals and other school leaders, who are learning the art and science of the "three-minute walk-through" advocated by the research, practice, and work of Downey, Steffy, English, Frase, and Poston (2004). The value of the three-minute walkthrough is acknowledged as a common practice; however, this book offers a different view of informal classroom observations. Namely, the informal classroom observation should be extended to more than three minutes to achieve its purposes—working with teachers in ways that are more meaningful.

The three-minute walkthrough serves to get principals out of their offices. Downey, Steffy, English, Frase, and Poston (2009) assert that the chief purpose of the three-minute walkthrough positions "the supervisory approach from a hierarchical inspection approach to one that is collaborative in motivating and promoting growth" (p. 1). The stance of this book is that a three-minute walkthrough is simply not enough time to capture a sustained picture of teaching and learning, and that is why this book advocates a more enlarged view of the informal classroom observation. In general, teachers want context-specific information about their teaching, and data observed in the window of a 15- to 20-minute observation can provide better opportunities for specific feedback, discussion, and reflection. What's there to talk about in a classroom observation that lasts a minute, or no longer than a television commercial?

Teaching and Learning to Teach Are Complex

Part of the process of learning to teach occurs in the overall school context and in the varying contexts of classrooms in which instruction unfolds in the presence of children. Learning to teach is mediated through such variables as preparation route (traditional or alternative certification), experience, professional development opportunities, and so on. Teaching is complex too. Regardless of how long one has been teaching, there is always room for improvement and professional growth. Because teaching is a lifetime pursuit, job-embedded learning opportunities should be provided for teachers to foster their professional growth.

Informal Teacher Observations Support Job-Embedded Learning

Informal teacher observations and follow-up postobservation conferences are important job-embedded learning strategies because teachers and leaders can purposefully learn from "their work activities" (Wood & Killian, 1998, p. 52). Hunzicker (2010) asserted, "Effective professional development for teachers is job-embedded, which makes it both relevant and authentic" (p. 4). Job-embedded professional development occurs during the school day and can be an individual or group/team experience. Collaborative or team job-embedded learning is especially effective (Nevills, 2003). It occurs during colleague discussions; team meetings; planning, mentoring and coaching sessions; action research projects; workshops; and other similar activities that teachers engage in daily. The final goal of job-embedded teacher professional development is improved student learning. Figure 1.1 (page 4) details the strengths of job-embedded learning.

FIGURE 1.1: Strengths of Job-Embedded Learning

Job-embedded learning:
- ♦ does not require participants to set aside a separate time to learn
- ♦ promotes immediate application of what is learned
- ♦ can be formal or informal
- ♦ links current information to previously learned information
- ♦ supports the generation of new ideas

Through classroom observations, teachers and leaders can link "learning and real-life problems" (Sparks & Hirsh, 1997, p. 52). As a job-embedded approach, informal classroom observations embrace what we know about the attributes of job-embedded learning:

1. Such learning adds relevance for teacher learning.

2. Feedback is built into the process.

3. The transfer of new skills into practice is facilitated (Zepeda, 2008).

Job-Embedded Learning Is More Relevant

Job-embedded learning is, by its very nature, relevant to the learner. Job-embedded learning addresses the goals and concerns of the individual teacher. In addition, job-embedded learning occurs at the teacher's job site and during the working day when the teacher is immersed in his or her work. Therefore, the teacher's learning becomes an integral part of the culture of the classroom and, by extension, the school.

Feedback Is Built into the Process of Job-Embedded Learning

In terms of informal observations as a type of job-embedded learning, we know that feedback is built into the process through the structure of the postobservation conference. The data collected during the classroom observation create fertile ground for ongoing discussions about teaching and learning. Teachers can use data to help see their classroom practices better. If informal classroom observations occur regularly during the course of a year, data can accumulate, and teachers can begin to use these data to chronicle implementation of new instructional skills, collect artifacts for assessing transitions from one learning activity to the next, and frame future classroom practices.

Job-Embedded Learning Facilitates the Transfer of New Skills into Practice

When ongoing support is linked with the lessons learned from classroom observations and time is afforded within the regular school day for teachers to make informed decisions based on data, transfer of skills into practice becomes part of the job. The research on job-embedded learning reports that it enhances reflection, promotes collegiality, combats isolation, makes learning more relevant to each teacher, targets the needs of adult learners, increases transfer of newly learned skills, impacts student achievement positively, supports the ongoing refinement of practice, and fosters a common lexicon that facilitates discussion and improvement among teachers.

Teachers learn to teach on the job through their experiences, as they plan for instruction and interact with their students. When teachers have the opportunity to talk about teaching, to share their insights, and to reflect on what occurs in the classroom, their learning increases. This type of job-embedded learning is enhanced through the efforts of the observant principal, supervisor, or coach who facilitates opportunities for teachers to reflect on and refine their practices through sustained feedback based on data from informal classroom observations.

Supervisors and Coaches Make the Commitment to Get Out and About

The overall intent of instructional supervision is teacher growth and development. Effective supervisors and coaches do not wait to be invited into classrooms; they find opportunities for informal visits, in addition to the more formal, mandated classroom observations tied to evaluation. They constantly scan the learning environment for ways to help teachers improve their talents.

Supervisors and coaches who find time to drop by classrooms seek and value opportunities to connect with their teachers and have a sincere desire to see teachers succeed as they face classroom challenges. Based on what supervisors and coaches observe in classrooms over time, they are able to:

♦ extend the talk about teaching and learning

♦ make purposeful efforts to promote whole-school involvement by sharing what others have learned

♦ foster a school-wide culture of concerted improvement

♦ involve others in conducting informal classroom observations, including members of the administrative team, department chairs, and teachers

♦ get creative about sharing what has been learned through faculty newsletters, electronic mailing lists, and video clips with promising teaching practices

♦ embed learning and professional development opportunities within the reality of the school's context

With a commitment to making informal classroom observations a part of the workday, these goals are achievable. Supervisors and coaches must wrap their thinking around the context of the school and the characteristics of the teachers in the building and then carve out time in an already busy and hectic workday to get into the classrooms and learn more about their teachers and those teachers' teaching styles. Effective supervisors and coaches "know their people."

Supervisors and Coaches Know Their People

Effective leaders do their homework up front, even before conducting their first informal classroom observation. These supervisors and coaches know their people, in part because they assess the characteristics of teachers; recognize teachers' career stages; assess teachers' willingness to learn; know, honor, and respect the adult learner; and assess individual teachers.

Assessing the Characteristics of Teachers

It is important for every school leader to systematically collect data about every teacher on a team. Tool 1 will assist school leaders in broadly profiling any given faculty. By gathering statistical information about a school's faculty, supervisors and coaches can begin to reflect on teachers' learning needs. It might be useful to have a faculty roster and a seniority list (typically available from the district office) to help track and tally information.

Tool 1   Assessing the Broad Characteristics of a Faculty

Purpose: Broadly assess the characteristics of a faculty

1. Number of teachers = 103   Male = 42   Female = 61

2. For each teacher, tally the number of years in teaching.

    Total number of years of experience = 900

    Average years of faculty experience =   9

3. Number of teachers whose experience falls within the following service ranges:

    a.   1 –   3 years = 23

    b.   4 –   7 years = 45

    c.   8 – 11 years =   0

    d.   12 – 15 years = 15

    e.   16 – 19 years =   0

    f.   20+ years = 20

4. Number of first-year teachers = 11

5. Number of teachers who retire at the end of the current school year = 19

6. Wildcards:

    First-year teachers with experience = 0

    Alternatively certified teachers = 5

    Teachers returning to work after an extended leave = 2

    Other = 0

7. What overall patterns do you notice?

    About 20% of these teachers have 3 or fewer years of experience.

    About 50% of the teachers are at the midpoint of their careers.

    About 20% of the teachers are in the wind-down stage of their careers.

    About 18% of the teachers are going to retire at the end of the current school year; more than likely there will be an influx of less experienced teachers hired the following school year.

Recognizing Teachers' Career Stages

Regardless of experience, position, grade level, or subject area, learning to teach is a process that continues throughout one's career, and this is why instructional supervision is important. Teachers have learning needs that shift over time, signaling inexact stages of development. At one time, most teachers entered the profession immediately following a four-year preparation program. Now, many teachers who have had successful careers in other areas entered the profession through alternative certification routes. Suffice it to say, knowledge about teachers' career stages is important if supervisors and coaches want to work more effectively to improve instructional support through the informal classroom observation process.

Figure 1.2 provides inexact but useful ways of thinking about teachers' career stages. The types of professional development and support that teachers need at the beginnings of their careers are very different from those needed by teachers who are further along in their careers and from those needed by veteran teachers.

FIGURE 1.2: Teacher Career Stages and Developmental Needs

Stage	Name	Years in Field (Approximate)	Developmental Theory and Needs
1	Preservice	0	Trains and prepares for a profession
2	Induction	1–2	Survival stage: Seeks safety and desires to learn the day-to-day operations of the school and the complexities of facing new situations in the classroom
3	Competency	3–5	Mounting confidence in work, as well as understanding of the multifaceted role of teaching
4	Enthusiasm	5–8	High job satisfaction stage: Actively seeks professional development and other opportunities
5	Career frustration	Varies	Burns out
6	Stability	Varies	Complacency stage: Experiences low innovation
7	Career wind-down	Varies	Coasts on past laurels and status with little effort required
8	Career exit	Varies	Ends teaching career

Adapted from Burden (1982); Burke, Christensen, and Fessler (1984); Christensen, Burke, Fessler, and Hagstrom (1983); Feiman and Floden (1980); Huberman, 1993; Katz, 1972.

Throughout an educator's career span, Burden (1982) found that many changes occur in the following areas:

♦ job skills, knowledge, and behavior—in areas such as teaching methods, discipline strategies, and curriculum planning

♦ attitudes and outlooks—in areas such as images of teaching, professional confidence and maturity, and willingness to try new teaching methods

♦ job events—in areas such as changes in grade level, school, or district; involvement in additional professional responsibilities; and age of entry and retirement (pp. 1–2)

Given this range, it is logical for supervisors and coaches to use informal classroom observation as a tool to assist teachers with the uncertainties they face as a result of these changes. These changes can also affect teachers' willingness to learn.

Assessing Teachers' Willingness to Learn

People learn at their own pace. Workplace conditions, such as the relationship between administration and teachers and the norms of collegiality, also affect learning. Learning can be neither mandated nor imposed. Adults respond to learning opportunities differently. Just as effective teachers know when to shift instruction and learning activities to meet the individual and collective needs of students, supervisors and coaches can be more effective if they know their teachers as "learners." From this perspective, supervisors and coaches are encouraged to view the school as a classroom in which all members are engaged in learning individually and collectively. Supervisors and coaches are able to assess current practices by examining the following:

♦ *Learning*: Do teachers seek out learning opportunities offered at the site, district, or externally, such as graduate school, local and national conferences, and workshops?

♦ *Sharing*: Do teachers share their knowledge and expertise with other teachers? Do teachers meet to share what they have learned in professional development activities?

♦ *Reflecting and discussing*: Do teachers openly discuss what they have learned about their own teaching practices? Are they provided with the time to reflect?

♦ *Examining the talk over time*: Are discussions held over sustained periods? One-time discussions do little to promote professional growth; continual discussion about progress and setbacks promotes personal and professional development.

♦ *Reading the word*: Are books, professional journals, and technology used as resources? Are these resources readily available and shared?

After examining these conditions, supervisors and coaches can further ready themselves for conducting informal classroom observations by understanding teachers as adult learners.

Knowing, Honoring, and Respecting the Adult Learner

Although this book is limited in its coverage of the principles of adult learning, there are several assumptions about adult learning that serve as a baseline for helping supervisors and coaches work more effectively with teachers.

Supervisors and coaches who promote adult development strive to make learning experiences self-directed, with the learner at the center of all activities; collaborative; supportive of trust, reflection, and open exchanges; problem-centered; applicable to their needs and job environment; and ongoing, as well as sustained (Brookfield, 1986; Knowles, 1973, 1980; Knowles, Swanson, & Holton, 2011).

Getting out of the office and entering the classroom to observe teachers is an important way to honor teachers' work and to help them to grow as adult learners. Supervisors and coaches who become welcomed guests in the classroom do so not by directing or being critical of the teacher, but by forming a partnership with the teacher. The value of supervisors and coaches getting out and about lies in the opportunity to provide teachers with occasions to reflect on their classroom practices through the objective data collected in informal observations. The power that results from this feedback and the dialogue it encourages is examined in Chapter 5 and Chapter 6.

Assessing Individual Teachers

Once a leader has a broad profile of the faculty, he or she can start planning future classroom observations. Despite the importance of the broad faculty profile, it does not provide enough information about every individual teacher. For informal classroom observations to be effective, supervisors and coaches should consider the learning needs of every teacher. It is a good idea to organize the information about every teacher in a consistent format that will give a principal, supervisor, or coach a quick overview of every teacher prior to planning classroom observation. Tool 2 presents a possible way to organize such data.

Tool 2   Assessing Individual Teachers

Purpose: Broadly assess individual teachers

1. Teacher's name: *Jane Adams*
2. Years in education: *25*
3. Years in the current position: *10*
4. Years in the current school: *10*
5. Teacher's career stage (circle one):
    a. Preservice
    b. Induction
    c. Competency
    d. Enthusiasm
    e. Career frustration
    (f.) Stability
    g. Career wind-down
    h. Career exit
6. Alternatively certified? If yes, in what area? *NO*
7. Other notes:

This tool was developed by Oksana Parylo, a doctoral student at the University of Georgia, Athens. Used with permission.

This information can be extended based on the classroom observation data. It is recommended that leaders keep a separate file for every teacher's observational data. The assessment of individual data (preserved with the assistance of Tool 2) can be the top sheet in a teacher's observational file, so leaders can update this information and/or extend information as needed. This tool is especially useful for leaders with a large staff of teachers or for leaders who are new to the school and do not yet know their staff well.

Leaders Assess the Context of Supervision and Their Own Beliefs

Teachers want accessible, visible leaders; they do not simply want open-door policies or mobile principals in the halls during passing periods. Teachers want principals, supervisors, and coaches to visit them in their classrooms, and they desire constructive feedback. Assessment of the context of supervision includes understanding the history of supervision and evaluation; knowing the intent and purpose of supervision and evaluation; and reflecting on the interactions, past and present, between teachers and supervisors or coaches. These factors shape the environment in which supervision evolves.

To create the conditions for effective informal classroom observations, leaders need to reflect on the nature of the interactions that surround supervisory practices. Leaders can assess the nature of prior classroom observations by asking, answering, and then reflecting on the meanings that their responses hold for the following questions:

- Are teachers used to seeing me and other administrators in their classrooms beyond the mandated classroom observations used to evaluate?

- Do teachers welcome me into their classrooms?

- What observation tools and techniques do I use?

- Do I merely report what I observe?

- Do I try to link other activities, such as professional development, to the supervisory process?

- Do I provide constructive and meaningful feedback?

- Are postobservation conferences conducted in a timely manner?

- Where are pre- and postobservation conferences conducted? (In the teacher's classroom? The main office?)

- Have I seen any positive changes in teachers or in the school overall that may have resulted from my classroom observations?

Learning and refining existing supervisory skills are ongoing practices that continually evolve as one gains experience and nurtures working relationships with teachers.

Supervisors and coaches often work with other site administrators and teacher leaders who should be a part of the supervisory efforts. Principals and other school leaders are encouraged to spend time nurturing administrative team members and others by conducting informal classroom observations.

Principals Develop the Leadership Skills of the Administrative Team

Given the size of many schools, it is almost impossible to expect a principal to stand alone, conducting all informal classroom observations. Although there is no substitute for the principal's visible presence in classrooms, there is a need for the administrative team to engage in the work of informal classroom observations. This involvement will multiply efforts, and, by including members of the administrative team and other school leaders, the principal creates important conditions to promote dialogue, affirm teachers' strengths, assist teachers in identifying areas of instruction that need improvement, target areas for professional development, and encourage reflection.

Before this can take place, however, members of the administrative team need to be informed and prepared to take on this responsibility. A solid beginning point is to understand the beliefs, values, and assumptions that the administrative team holds regarding teaching, learning, and making the efforts needed to support teachers through informal classroom observations. These understandings are important, because an administrative team that operates with similar beliefs, values, and assumptions sends a unified and powerful message to teachers.

As the leader, the principal is encouraged to set aside time for sustained discussion, so that administrative team members can collectively explore their responses to the following open-ended statements:

- As a team, we plan for ...
- As a team, we monitor ...
- As a team, we model ...
- As a team, we recognize and celebrate ...
- As a team, we are willing to confront ...
- As a team, we believe effective teachers are those who ...
- As a team, we believe an effective classroom is one in which ...
- As a team, we believe effective feedback is ...
- As a team, we believe teachers grow professionally by ...
- As a team, we support teaching and learning by ...

Without such introspection, a school's administrative team will not be synchronized to work alongside the principal to meet the needs of teachers. An administrative team that works together can build a unified vision for supervision and professional development, create a healthy learning culture, serve as valuable resources to help teachers meet their needs, coordinate and provide appropriate learning opportunities based on these needs, and grow as professionals from their work in the school.

Making informal classroom observations an administrative priority takes concerted effort on the part of the principal and the administrative team. It takes time to make informal classroom observations a habit of mind and practice. Such a commitment is really a commitment to the overall improvement of the instructional program that focuses on the efforts of teachers but is dependent, in part, on the following tasks of the administrative team:

- *Redefining relationships with each other and with teachers.* This process begins with the principal flattening the hierarchical structures within leadership teams (e.g., principal, associate principal, assistant principal, deans, instructional deans, department chairs, lead teachers, and grade-level coordinators).

- *Sharing responsibility for learning.* All team members need to assume an active role in providing learning opportunities for themselves as they work with teachers.

- *Creating an atmosphere of interdependence.* Each member of the team needs to feel a sense of belonging, contributing to individual and collective learning opportunities while working alongside fellow administrative team members and teachers.

- *Making time for professional development.* Time is often cited as the main reason principals and other members of the administrative team cannot function as instructional leaders. Consider the reaction teachers might receive if they indicated that they did not have time to make it to class or correct student work.

- *Developing a plan for professional development, with teacher needs guiding the process.* No plan that is not grounded in the needs of its learners will yield significant results.

- *Rotating responsibilities.* Rotation of specific duties and responsibilities associated with professional development can help get all members of the administrative team on the same proverbial page. This rotation can also assist with breaking down barriers between people within the organization while supporting the development of skills and expertise for all team members.

- *Linking school-wide initiatives.* The coordination of school initiatives will reduce unnecessary duplication of programs and provide resources to support initiatives.

Supervisors and Coaches Develop Practices to Track Observation Efforts

Informal observations should be tracked. Tool 3 provides an example of how supervisors and coaches can track the informal classroom observations. By reviewing the record of formal and informal classroom observations, supervisors and coaches can determine whether any teachers were missed; whether observations were spread evenly throughout the day, indicated by the period or time of the observation, as well as the year; what follow-up topics were discussed; and when the postobservation conferences occurred. Supervisors and coaches can also look for patterns. For example, in Tool 3, Marlowe did not observe Baker for four months, and there was a nearly two-week delay in the follow-up; Linton balanced formal and informal observations; and Schmidt did not engage Burton in any follow-up to the informal classroom observations. Supervisors and coaches should interpret these patterns in the context of the school and the characteristics of the teachers being supervised.

Tool 3   Tracking Informal Observations

Purpose: Keep a record of the conducted informal classroom observations

Teacher	Observer	Informal Observations	Date of Follow-Up	Formal Observations	Period(s)/ Time(s)	Follow-Up Topics
Adams	Schmidt	9/04/2011 11/03/2011	9/05/2011 11/04/2011	10/06/2011	1 (8:15-8:30) 5 (11:10-11:20)	Cooperative learning grouping
Baker	Marlowe	11/07/2011 3/05/2012	11/10/2011 3/16/2012	3/20/2011	1 (8:15-8:25)	Instructional pacing
Beatty	Linton	9/05/2011 9/08/2011 10/20/2011 11/12/2011	9/08/2011 9/08/2011 10/21/2011 11/14/2011	10/07/2011 10/14/2011 11/03/2011 11/26/2011	1 (8:30-8:45) 3 (10:10-10:25) 1 (8:15-8:25) 6 (1:05-1:15)	Classroom management; beginning- and end-of-period procedures
Burton	Schmidt	9/08/2011 11/20/2011	None None	10/31/2011	1 (8:00-8:15) 8 (2:15-2:30)	Classroom management

Looking Ahead...

Chapter 2 details the intent of informal classroom observations and the premise behind informal classroom observations and provides some basic guidelines to consider while engaging in informal classroom observations.

2
Framing Informal Classroom Observations

In This Chapter...

♦ Supervisors and coaches understand the intent of teacher observation and instructional supervision.

♦ Principals utilize the various methods of informal classroom observations.

♦ Leaders link informal classroom observations to school-wide instructional improvement efforts.

♦ Supervisors and coaches know the guidelines for informal classroom observations.

This chapter includes tools designed to help supervisors and coaches emerge as leaders while conducting informal classroom observations. The following tools are offered:

To endure, a supervisory program that includes informal classroom observations that go beyond hit and miss requires an understanding of the intents of teacher observation and supervision. Informal classroom observations need to be based on guidelines to bolster teacher learning and development, and they should not be viewed or conducted as a "drive-through" in which an observer blitzes in and out of the classroom without offering feedback. The drive-through approach does not give the observer enough time to capture the events of the classroom, collect data that are stable, or provide enough hooks to engage the teacher in reflective discussions.

The Intent of Teacher Observation and Instructional Supervision

Observing teachers in action is the primary method of assessing teaching. Through formal and informal classroom observations, supervisors and coaches gain insights into classroom practices: instructional strategies; learning activities, including performance assessments; the taught curriculum; and the types of teacher-student interactions that evolve throughout the course of instruction. Informal classroom observations are a part of the overall supervising program that promotes teacher development and growth, interaction between teachers and administrators, fault-free problem solving, and building teacher capacity (Zepeda, 2007).

Both instructional supervision and informal classroom observations are formative assessments that lead to teacher growth and development and, by extension, to improved student learning.

Effective classroom observations support the overall instructional program and the teachers who deliver it. Classroom observations also signal to teachers that the supervisor or coach cares about the teachers and the work they do. The classroom presence of a supervisor or coach promotes a healthy climate and creates conditions for the ongoing discussion, reflection, and refinement of existing practices, as well as adoption of new teaching practices.

Both Teachers and Observers Benefit from Classroom Observations

Classroom observations, whether formal or informal, provide opportunities for both the observer and the teacher to develop a broader range of understanding of the complexities of teaching and learning. For this range of understanding to emerge, classroom observations must occur over time with sustained attention to the processes used to observe teachers (observation tools are examined in Chapter 4). Classroom observations provide opportunities *for teachers* to do the following:

♦ learn more about their teaching through the leader's support and presence

♦ extend talk about teaching and reduce feelings of isolation

♦ examine what works and which areas of instruction or classroom management could be enhanced by modifying practice

♦ receive affirmation of their instructional efforts

♦ gauge short- and long-term efforts by examining objective data collected over a sustained period of time

For observers, there are benefits and opportunities as well. *Observers* benefit from informal observations because they

♦ learn more about teaching and learning and their teachers

♦ share alternative strategies observed in other classrooms with teachers

♦ frame professional development opportunities for teachers across grade levels and subject areas

- obtain a deeper understanding of the complexities of the classroom, as well as how teachers handle these complexities

- lend assistance to teachers who have needs

- gain more than snapshot views of teachers

- enhance the supervisory and evaluation plan at the given site

The intent of supervision is to improve teaching and to lend assistance to teachers as they move through their careers. To this end, supervision is a proactive, ongoing set of processes and procedures.

Utilization of Informal Classroom Observations

Every school system has processes in place for formal teacher evaluations that are based on state statutes regarding evaluation, union agreements, and other context-specific factors that make each school system unique. It is wise to know system-wide policies and procedures, along with the history of supervision at the site. The way that informal observations are conducted will dictate teachers' willingness to embrace this practice as an ongoing component of professional learning and job-embedded professional development.

Management by Wandering Around

Informal classroom observation has evolved in the literature and in practice. Recently, there has been resurgence in attention to informal classroom observation. The popularity of informal classroom observation can be tied to the *management by wandering around* (MBWA) movement, popularized by Peters and Waterman (1982) in their book *In Search of Excellence: Lessons from America's Best Run Companies.* The MBWA movement originated in the business world and the original book promoting this approach (Peters & Waterman, 1982) was grounded on the best executive practices of business leaders like Hewlett Packard, Coca Cola, and others. MBWA suggests that executives make unannounced visits to employees; visit all employees; have employees talk about unrelated topics like their families, friends, or hobbies; let employees show their skills; encourage all employees; watch/observe, listen, and ask questions; and avoid criticizing performance.

Executives who embraced MBWA promoted informal communication and personal involvement with employees by getting out of the office. Through this accessibility and visibility, executives were able to ensure accountability and affirm the work of employees. The practice of informal classroom observations also embraces getting supervision and evaluation out of the main office, situating observers as active participants in the instructional lives of their teachers by promoting visibility and accessibility.

Walking-Around Supervision and Short Visits

In the supervision and teacher evaluation literature, informal classroom observations have been tied to both formative and summative evaluation practices. Manning (1988) asserted that information about teachers gleaned from "walking-around supervision" and "short visits" should be included as summative samplings in the overall evaluation of teaching. Although the two are similar, Manning makes a sharp distinction between walking-around supervision and short visits. Walking-around supervision promotes the visibility of the principal or other leaders, primarily in the lunchrooms, "in the halls…before and after the first bell in the morning, and immediately before the dismissal bell in the afternoon" (p. 145). During these and other times, the principal, supervisor, or coach collects information about instruction and plans short visits, if there is a need (e.g., a teacher who is having difficulties with classroom management or a teacher who is regarded as having an exemplary instructional method).

According to Manning, short visits last longer than walking-around visits, typically "less than a full class period." Also, "it is important to always follow up a short visit with a brief conference," especially "if a problem is noted, the principal can discuss this…and plan for an additional evaluation" (p. 146). Manning's position is aligned with the premises of instructional supervision—to be effective and bring about desired results, every observation should be followed by a postobservation conference that provides an opportunity for a teacher and an observer to discuss the part of the lesson that was observed, analyze the data collected by the observer, and take any necessary steps for future improvement.

Catch Teachers in the Act of Teaching

A supervisor or coach does not conduct informal classroom visitations to catch the teacher off guard or to interrupt classroom activities. Informal classroom observations allow supervisors and coaches to affirm what teachers are doing right by encouraging them to keep up the momentum. The data collected in a classroom observation may help teachers improve their teaching practices by providing information about their teaching. Moreover, informal observations allow the observer and teacher to celebrate successes in teaching and student learning.

Informal observations are one way instructional supervisors can get to know their teachers. By observing teachers' work in their classrooms, supervisors or coaches can exert informed effort and energy to assist teachers beyond formally scheduled observations. Informal observations provide opportunities for supervisors to motivate teachers, monitor instruction, be accessible and provide support, and keep informed about instruction in the school (Blase & Blase, 1998, pp. 108–109).

An Observation by Any Other Name

Sometimes referred to as *pop-ins*, *walk-ins*, or *drop-ins*, informal classroom observations have the following characteristics:

+ They are brief, lasting approximately 15–20 minutes (perhaps longer).

+ They are unannounced, in most cases.

+ They can occur at the beginning, middle, or end of a class period.

+ They can occur at any time during the school day.

+ They are conducted with a sole purpose of helping teachers develop and grow.

+ They focus on a variety of aspects, including, but not limited to, instruction, use of time, classroom management, transitions between learning activities, and the clarity of instructions.

Informal classroom observation is a strategy for getting into classrooms, with the intent of focusing on teaching, learning, and the interactions between teachers and students as the events of instruction unfold. As a strategy, the Center for Comprehensive School Reform and Improvement (2007) reports:

> The walk-through can be defined as a brief, structured non-evaluative classroom observation by the principal that is followed by a conversation between the principal and the teacher about what was observed. Used well, the walk-through can provide both principal and teacher with valuable information about the status of the school's instructional program. (p. 1)

Informal classroom observations are nonevaluative in nature. Observers cannot expect teachers to openly share their teaching issues during the informal conversations, if there is risk that this information could be used in a punitive manner. Informal observations are incomplete without a debriefing conference or meeting in which the teacher and observer have a chance to discuss what was observed.

A promising practice emerging in the field is the learning walk. The learning walk is done by a team that consists of teachers, teacher leaders, and administrators who target grade levels or subject areas to conduct brief, seven- to 10-minute classroom observations as teams. In addition to school personnel, external observers (i.e., teachers from other schools or parents) can be members of the learning-walk teams. The focus of the learning walk is to examine how teachers teach and how students learn. Like other types of short classroom observation visits, learning walks are nonevaluative and are aimed at teacher improvement.

There is typically a focus for the learning walk—questioning strategies, wait time, variety of instructional strategies, classroom management, cooperative learning, differentiated instruction, and so on. The group conducts the learning walk, debriefs about the data for a few minutes, and then, as a group, goes into another classroom for seven to 10 minutes, debriefs, and continues the cycle. One possible strategy is to divide a larger team into pairs that will visit different classrooms. In this scenario, the pairs have a short debrief after visiting every classroom, and an overall debrief is held at the end of the day. At the end of the day, the walk teams summarize the data and then engage in conversations with the teachers whose classrooms were observed.

We briefly analyzed different types of informal observations: management by walking around; walking around supervision and short visits; and pop-ins, walk-ins, or drop-ins. Although slightly different in the way they are conducted, these types of informal classroom observations have the same characteristics:

- They have short duration.
- They are typically unannounced.
- They are nonevaluative in nature.
- They aim to promote teacher development and growth.
- They are followed up by a conversation between the teacher and the observer.

Informal observations are not intended to supplant formal observations; they have different purposes and do not include a preobservation conference. Too often, however, informal classroom observations also forgo postobservation conferences. The value of the informal observation, which culminates with an opportunity to talk with teachers, is that observers can strengthen their relationships with teachers by communicating something about what was observed. In fact, a majority of informal observations should include some type of follow-up conversation about teaching and learning. Chapter 4 details tools that can be used to chronicle what is observed during informal classroom observations, and Chapter 5 offers techniques for communicating what is observed, along with strategies to assist teachers in reflecting on their practices. Chapter 6 provides insights on how supervisors and coaches can engage teachers in discussion about student work.

How Much Time Is Enough?

The interest in informal classroom observations was piqued by the Downey Informal Observation method in which principals spend three to five minutes observing a classroom (Downey, Steffy, English, Frase, & Poston, 2004). Although that method certainly gets supervision out of the main office, the principal (or any observer) is encouraged to spend more than three to five minutes in the classroom so that the observer and teacher have a meaningful experience. The brevity of the egg-timer approach to classroom observation minimizes data collection. It is preferable to conduct fewer, but longer, informal observations on a daily basis. This extra time pays short- and long-term dividends—connecting with teachers, while deriving a more accurate sense of the classroom activities observed, and movement toward high-quality learning for the teachers entrusted to educate children.

One of any school leader's daily struggles is to find time for mandatory formal classroom observations and informal classroom visits. Although no clear-cut solution to this problem applies across all school systems, many leaders have found creative ways to make the most of their available human resources and provide a supervisory program centered on teachers' needs. Chapter 1 discussed cues to include the administrative team with informal classroom observations. A commitment to being more visible to teachers is strengthened by the impact that classroom visitations can have on bolstering the instructional program.

Linking Informal Observations to School-Wide Instructional Improvement Efforts

It is not uncommon for schools to identify an instructional focus and targeted strategies for the year. For leaders who work with their teachers to identify instructional strategies to master during the year, informal classroom observations can be instrumental in helping the observer provide focused feedback. Because the observer gets out and about, he or she has the opportunity to see first-hand instructional efforts toward implementing strategies. During postobservation conferences, the observer has the opportunity to help teachers reflect on how these strategies are being implemented, provide the forum for joint exploration on refining instructional practices, and affirm the work teachers are doing to help students learn.

At Creekland Middle School (Lawrenceville, GA, Gwinnett County Public Schools), former principal Dr. Bill Kruskamp and the 170 teachers agreed to spend a year mastering six strategies, assess how these strategies were being implemented and refined, and then move forward with identifying more strategies to build on the original six strategies:

- ♦ Collaboration

- ♦ Differentiation

- ♦ Student Engagement

- ♦ Summarizing

- ♦ Display of Student Work

- ♦ Essential Question (EQ)

With close to 3,000 students at Creekland Middle School (at the time of this initiative), the largest middle school in the state of Georgia and one of the largest in the United States, the administrative team was aware that they had to make informal classroom observations purposeful and that they had to take every opportunity to connect the work of teachers to the overall school-wide instructional improvement efforts. To ensure that informal classroom observations focused on the six strategies, Bill Kruskamp and the six assistant principals developed their own informal classroom observation tools (see Tool 4 and Tool 5, page 22).

Throughout the year, the administrative team debriefed to learn, as a collective, what was occurring instructionally at Creekland Middle School. From their discussions, professional development was geared toward assisting teachers' master skills and then toward focusing, and in some instances refocusing, their attention during subsequent informal classroom observations. Tool 5 illustrates a focus on the relationship between the essential question and answer summarizing.

A treasure chest of classroom observation tools suitable for the informal classroom observation is offered in Chapter 3 and Chapter 4.

Guidelines for Informal Classroom Observations

The following guidelines for informal classroom observations are offered as a starting point for framing this important work.

Informally Observe All Teachers

All teachers can benefit from informal classroom observation. Refrain, however, from "overobserving" particular teachers (e.g., only teachers having difficulty, beginning teachers, teachers who teach subject areas that are heavily tested). Informal classroom observation should last between 15 and 20 minutes; therefore, conduct only as many observations in a day as can be followed up on with a postobservation conference either the same day or the next day. Teachers need and deserve some type of immediate feedback.

Informally Observe as Often as Possible

The presence of a principal, supervisor, or coach in classrooms sends a positive message to teachers: the leadership of the school cares. Including informal classroom observation as a school-wide initiative requires consistency and frequency. Become opportunistic in finding time in the day to observe teachers, and vary the time of day in which observation occurs. What occurs in the morning is much different from what occurs in the afternoon.

Tool 4   Focused Informal Classroom Observations— Creekland Middle School

Angle: Narrow

Focus: Instructional strategies and classroom expectations

Teacher: *Lori Miller*   **Date:** *March 14, 2011*

Administrator: *Bill Kruskamp*   **Class Period:** *4th*

Common Classroom Expectations:

- collaboration
- differentiation
- student engagement

- summarizing
- display of student work
- essential questions (EQ)

Expectation Domains	Presence = X
1. **Assessment:** Frequently assesses students' learning of the AKS and gives specific feedback to the students and parents.	
2. **Nonverbal Representations:** Uses a variety of nonverbal/visual representations of content and skills.	
3. **Modeling and Practice:** Models strategies and skills. Provides multiple opportunities for distributed practice, followed by independent practice.	X
4. **Vocabulary:** Explicitly teaches essential content-related vocabulary.	
5. **Summarizing:** Explicitly teaches students to summarize their learning.	X
6. **Collaboration:** Provides collaborative learning opportunities.	
7. **Student Goal Setting:** Teaches and requires students to set personal goals for improving their academic achievement.	
8. **Literacy:** Explicitly teaches skills for improving reading and writing proficiency/ literacy across the content areas.	
9. **Problem Solving:** Uses inquiry-based, problem-solving learning strategies with students in all content areas.	
10. **Questioning:** Uses and teaches questioning and cuing/ prompting techniques.	X
11. **Background Knowledge:** Accesses and/or builds students' background knowledge and experiences.	
12. **Comparison and Contrast:** Teaches students to compare and contrast knowledge, concepts, and content.	
13. **Technology:** Uses technology effectively to plan, teach, and assess.	

Comments:

Lori: Getting to higher-order questions supported your assessment in two ways: (1) students summarized what they had learned and (2) students were "stretched" to answer questions that showed mastery of content. For example, you asked, "What is democracy?" Then you asked students to identify democratic practices in local politicians, and then you asked students, "How do you apply democratic principles in your everyday life?" I enjoyed the classroom observation. I will look for some materials that I may have regarding democracy that may help you.

Used with permission. Dr. Bill Kruskamp, former principal, Creekland Middle School, Gwinnett County Public Schools (Lawrenceville, GA).

Tool 5   Informal Classroom Observation: Essential Question and Answer Summarizing—Creekland Middle School

Angle: Narrow

Focus: Essential question and answer summarizing

Teacher: Andy Bercher   **Date:** March 27, 2011

Essential questions (circle one):   (Yes)   No

- posted
- guided instruction
- used at the end of lessons to assist summarizing and gathering evidence of learning

Summarizing (circle one):   (Yes)   No

- reflects evidence of student learning
- all students participate
- guided by the essential question

What were the students doing?

Students were working in pairs with <u>manipulatives</u> as they solved algebraic equations.

Comments:

Andy, you really had the students engaged in this lesson! When students reported out from their groups, it was clear that they were able to summarize their learning about balancing the two sides of the equation. I look forward to seeing where this lesson continues and students gain mastery.

Thanks—Bill

Used with permission. Dr. Bill Kruskamp, former principal, Creekland Middle School, Gwinnett County Public Schools (Lawrenceville, GA).

Watch, Listen, and Write, But Focus on One or Two Areas

Although there is no predetermined focus established, because there is no preobservation conference, find a focus based on the instruction, events, or discussions that are occurring in the classroom. As much as possible, avoid publicizing personal biases that may encourage teachers to "play to the audience." For example, if the observer is a proponent of cooperative learning, teachers might be tempted to transition to cooperative learning activities once the observer enters the room.

Given that informal observations are relatively brief (15–20 minutes) compared to extended classroom observations (30–45 minutes), data from a single focus will make richer conversation during follow-up discussion.

Let It Be Obvious that You Are Having Fun

An observer's demeanor sends strong messages: either the principal, supervisor, or coach enjoys being out and about or he or she grudgingly engages in informal classroom observations. Let your body language and facial expressions communicate that you are enjoying the time in the classroom. Think about how you want teachers and students to view you.

Catch Them in the Act of Doing Something Right and Applaud Efforts

Look for victories, rather than failures, and applaud them. Work to create an ethos of sharing. Teachers especially adept at a strategy or technique need time and opportunities for sharing their expertise with others. For example, a certain amount of time at weekly or monthly faculty meetings could be set aside for teachers to share insights or techniques with one another.

Make the Time to Follow Up

Follow-up communication to informal classroom observation is a critical component. Through conversations and reflection, teachers better understand the complexities of their work. Feedback and dialogue form the cornerstone of all supervisory activities.

Follow Up with Resources

After feedback, an effective observer also makes available resources that teachers need to refine practice. The observer's efforts to return for a follow-up informal observation might be one such resource.

Make Informal Observations Invitational

Encourage teachers to invite you to observe them. Teachers experimenting with novel instructional approaches or whose students are making presentations would welcome the opportunity for the principal, supervisor, or coach to be present (FutureCents, 2005).

Looking Ahead...

Chapter 3 explores the intent of data collection and offers broad techniques to consider before exploring and applying the classroom observation tools presented in Chapter 4.

3

Understanding Data-Collection Techniques and Approaches

In This Chapter...

- ♦ Supervisors and coaches understand the intent of data collection.
- ♦ Leaders know data sources.
- ♦ Observers are familiar with the types of data.
- ♦ Supervisors and coaches use data-collection techniques.

This chapter includes tools designed to help supervisors and coaches emerge as leaders while conducting informal classroom observations. The following tools are offered:

One word frequently used around the topic of observations is data. Observers collect data, handle data, analyze data, and systematize data. Teachers are told to organize student data, achievement data, demographic data, and other data. Data seem to be important to everyone in a school system. But what are data? For the purposes of this book, data are defined as any measurable or perceptual information about the students, teachers, community, and school system. Data can come from formal sources (Census data, school report cards, etc.) or informal sources (e.g., informal classroom observations).

Fertile data can be gleaned from an informal classroom observation lasting between 15 and 20 minutes. More than merely watching during an informal observation, the observer collects stable and useful data. Accurate and bias-free data further assists teachers in making sense of their teaching. The intent of data collection, data sources, and data-collection techniques is examined in this chapter, and in Chapter 4 the data-collection tools used during classroom observations are applied.

The Intents of Data Collection

The adage "less is more" is worth exploring, given that an informal classroom observation lasts a relatively short time. Brevity, coupled with the fast-paced nature of activities in a classroom, dictates that the observer focus on less to provide a more detailed and richer portrayal of what occurred. Many types of data can be collected during an informal classroom observation. Consider the possibilities:

♦ engagement of the learner through the content

♦ instructional methods used to deliver the content

♦ types of activities that engage learners

♦ the types of questions asked by a teacher and/or students

♦ resources used to enhance learning experiences

♦ types of assessments used to make judgments about learning

These areas are important to teaching and learning, and all deserve attention. According to McGreal (1988), there are four presuppositions of data collection that should drive observations and the tools used to collect data:

1. The reliability and usefulness of classroom observation is related to the amount and types of information that supervisors have prior to the observation.

2. The narrower the focus that supervisors use in observing classrooms, the more likely they will be to describe the events related to that focus.

3. The impact of observational data is related to the way the data are recorded during the observation.

4. The impact of observational data on supervisor-teacher relationships is related to the way feedback is presented to the teacher. (pp. 21–22)

The first presupposition applies more readily to a formal classroom observation that includes a preobservation conference in which the teacher and observer agree on a focus

FIGURE 3.1: Focus Areas for Informal Classroom Observations

Broad Focus Area	Possible Target Points Within the Focus Area
Instructional methods and techniques	cooperative learning, direct instruction, indirect instruction, questioning strategies, wait time
Organizing for instruction	use of advance organizers; posing a problem, dilemma, or objective
Classroom procedures	beginning and ending classroom procedures, transitions, physical proximity, and movement
Student engagement and involvement	on- and off-task behavior, questioning strategies, use of student responses to extend discussion, maintaining student focus and attention
Subject matter and content	organization, breadth, depth, and scope
Other	use of technology and manipulatives

for the classroom observation. The predetermined focus drives the classroom observation and the techniques used to collect data. In a formal classroom observation, a teacher and a principal, supervisor, or coach collectively decide on the observation purpose and data-collection technique; in this way, the informal classroom observation is different.

During an informal classroom observation, the observer develops a focus on the spot, and this is why the principal, supervisor, or coach is more than a mere observer. The principal, supervisor, or coach becomes a silent, but active, participant, making a snap judgment about what to focus on and for how long. The broad focus of the classroom observation is dependent on what occurs in the classroom. Figure 3.1 examines some possibilities that the principal, supervisor, or coach might focus on during an informal classroom observation.

Teaching is not an isolated enterprise; one area of instruction affects other areas (e.g., organizing for instruction affects student engagement). This is why the learning environment is exciting. Because teachers are engaged in the moments of teaching and make split-second decisions about what to do next based on student responses, they benefit from data, subsequent feedback, and opportunities to talk and reflect about teaching.

Data Sources

In supervision, the richest source of data comes from classroom observations. The information collected by the principal, supervisor, or coach during an observation is observational data. These data are typically phrases from the teacher and/or students that the observer jotted down during the observation. These data may also include the observer's categorization of what has occurred during an observation. An example of the categorization may be choosing the question level according to Bloom's Taxonomy or noting the presence or absence of some specific criteria that the observer looked for (see Tool 5 in Chapter 2).

In addition to observational data, there are also preexisting data that the observer should keep in mind while conducting an informal classroom observation. Figure 3.2 shows the relationship between the preexisting and observational data.

Informal Classroom Observations On the Go

FIGURE 3.2: Data Sources

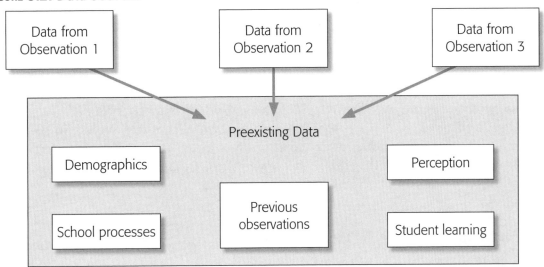

Note that, in Figure 3.2, the observational data areas are directed toward the preexisting data. All the data collected during classroom observations further enrich and enlarge the database of school leaders and the school in general.

The preexisting data come from internal (faculty surveys, student interviews, etc.) or external sources (the Department of Education of the State or US Census data). Bernhardt (2007) differentiated four groups of data: *demographic data* (i.e., enrollment, attendance, drop-out rate, ethnicity, gender, and grade level); *school processes data* (i.e., descriptions of school programs and processes); *perception data* (i.e., perceptions of learning environment, attitudes, and beliefs); and *student learning data* (i.e., standardized and criterion-referenced tests, as well as *authentic assessment).* These data come from multiple sources and are divided into three major types.

Types of Data

Data may be quantitative, qualitative, or a combination of both. *Quantitative* data include frequencies, distributions, and other counts or tallies of information (see Figure 3.3, page 28, and Figure 3.4, page 29). Checklists are quantitative because they do not use words to describe what, how, or why something occurred. For example, the observer could use a checklist to tally how many questions were asked of children in the front row or how many times the teacher called on students whose hands were raised or not raised. *Qualitative* data could include scripted notes, detailing patterns of activities, words, and other events observed (see Tool 8, page 34). Whether data are quantitative or qualitative, accuracy is essential; the credibility of the process and the observer is at stake.

Another related issue is data validity—the observer should be in a classroom for a long enough time to collect valid data. Therefore, it is unlikely that a three- to five-minute observation can yield valid data. Finally, *mixed* data combine both qualitative and quantitative data collected during a classroom observation (see Tool 14, page 42). An example of mixed data may be a checklist (quantitative) with additional fields to record teacher's questions, student responses, or classroom routines.

Types of Data and Data-Collecting Techniques

On entering the classroom, the observer makes two major decisions:

1. where to focus attention during the observation

2. what observation technique(s) is best suited to collect and display the data

These two considerations are interrelated because what the observer decides to focus on during the observation dictates which technique or tool is most suitable for collecting data. Regardless of the technique for data collection, always start small by focusing on one or two items, and take notes that relate directly to those items. Remember: less is more!

Figure 3.3 provides an overview of the techniques used to collect data while observing teachers.

Wide-Angle and Narrow-Angle Methods

Acheson and Gall (1997) and Gall and Acheson (2011) developed a series of data-collection tools that are classified as either wide-angle methods or narrow-angle methods, similar to the lenses available for use in a camera. In general, the wide-angle methods allow an observer to capture a larger picture, whereas the narrow-angle methods allow an observer to "zoom in" and collect more finite data focused on one or two aspects. Figure 3.4 describes the six most commonly used data-collection tools developed by Acheson and Gall (1997).

FIGURE 3.3: Classroom Observation Data-Collection Techniques

Techniques	Description
Behavior category	A narrow set of behaviors is tracked.
Checklist	A standardized form allows the principal to check which activities and behaviors are present or absent.
Classroom diagramming	Classroom tracking of certain behaviors or movement of teachers and students are recorded in short increments of time.
Selected verbatim notes	Words, questions, and interactions are recorded verbatim.
Open narrative	Anecdotal notes with or without a focus are recorded.
Teacher-designed instrument	Teacher develops an instrument to audit certain teaching and learning behaviors.
Audiotape	The principal audiotapes the class, often taking notes or diagramming movement; the audio recording can be used to help reconstruct the events of the lesson.
Videotape	The events of the classroom are videotaped and viewed at a later time.

FIGURE 3.4: Data-Collection Tools: An Overview of Methods

Type of Method/Lens	Data-Collection Tool	Focus
Narrow lens	Selective verbatim	Records words that were said by the teacher, the students, or both
Narrow lens	Verbal flow	Details the frequency of who spoke—how often and when
Narrow lens	At-task	Provides detail, noting periodically over time of who appears to be at-task
Narrow lens	Class traffic	Tracks the teacher's (or the students') physical movement
Narrow lens	Interaction analysis	Provides detail about the types of statements made by either the teacher or the students
Wide lens	Anecdotal/global scan	Notes what was occurring overall in the classroom and can become more subjective, unless the supervisor records "just the facts"

Adapted from Acheson and Gall (1997).

Narrow-Angle Methods and Tools

Narrow-angle data-collection methods have several tools, including selective verbatim, verbal flow, at-task, class traffic, and interaction analysis. These tools help the supervisor collect data that detail which students are engaged by focusing on very specific types of data: words, frequency of words, student or teacher movement, and so forth. For example, if the principal, supervisor, or coach enters a classroom in which the teacher engages students in a question-and-answer session, it is ideal to focus on what types of questions are asked. The observer narrows the observation technique to chronicle, in detail, the questions asked of students. Therefore, the observer needs to write, as verbatim as possible, the questions asked. The scope of data collected would typically be just the questions; however, the lens can widen to track not only the questions the teacher asks, but also the students' responses to the questions (see Figure 4.1, page 52).

Wide-Angle Methods and Tools

The most prevalent wide-angle tool is the global scan, which is useful for collecting information about the events of the class as they unfold. Data could include the words said by the teacher and students, the physical activity of the teacher and students, the types of instructional methods used and their duration—or just about any other event or occurrence in the classroom. The global scan is intended to give the teacher a general sense of the classroom.

The strength of the wide-angle method of recording anecdotally is the ability to chronicle events as they occur. A weakness is the possibility that bias and value judgment may emerge as the events are being scripted. Consider the following two statements:

Data Collection

1. "While you were giving instructions for the small-group activity, one girl left her seat to sharpen a pencil."

2. "Your instructions were unclear, so students tuned out. One girl began sharpening her pencil while you were talking, an effort to undercut your authority."

The first statement presents the facts without editorial speculation. The second statement is value laden; even its wording (i.e., "tuned out" and "undercut your authority") sends a negative message. How is the teacher likely to respond to each statement? Using the wide-angle method of scripting anecdotally requires a conscious effort to leave value judgments off the page.

Data Are Important Because...

Data collected during classroom observations tend to describe teacher and student behaviors using a series of snapshots, with each piece of data depicting isolated events that occurred during a teaching episode. It is the analysis of the data that permits the teacher and the supervisor to identify patterns through which a holistic image of teaching can be created. The key for success is to observe not only the teacher, but also the students. Effective observation involves keeping one eye on the teacher and the other eye on the students, tracking the effect of teaching behaviors on student response and learning.

Show Me the Data!

Each data-collection tool has its strengths and limitations and yields different types of information about the events of the classroom observation. The following illustrates what data would look like, using select data-collection tools described in Figure 3.4.

Selective verbatim focuses on specific words, questions, or responses made by the teacher, students, or both. The first example focuses on the questions the teacher asks.

T: What were the events leading up to the crime?
T: Of these events, which event motivated the main character the most?
T: Why was this event the most important?
T: How would the ending of the book have been different if this event had not occurred?

The next example displays both the teacher's questions and the student's responses to the questions.

Teacher Questions	Student Responses
1. What were the events leading up to the crime?	1. The man was desperate; he had to feed his children; he lost his job; his oldest son was diagnosed with a life-threatening disease.
2. Of these events, which event motivated the main character the most?	2. The son's life-threatening disease.
3. Why was this event the most important?	3. He had no money to pay the doctor.

Tool 6   Selective Verbatim: Praise, Correction, and Preventive Prompts

Angle: Narrow

Focus: Teacher's skills in giving praise, correction, and preventive prompts

Teacher: Bob Bennett   **Observer:** Pat Montalvo

Date of Observation: February 25, 2011   **Start Time:** 9:40   **End Time:** 9:50

Total Observation Time: 10 minutes   **Period of the Day:** Morning

Number of Students Present: 11   **Grade Level:** Sophomore

Class: Study and Life Skills   **Topic of the Lesson:** Teacher was readying the class to begin work

Date of Postobservation Conference: February 26, 2011

Teacher Comment/Response	Time	Praise	Correction	Preventive Prompt
Please come in and get seated.	9:40			X
Bob, close the door and come in.	9:41		X	
Your pencils need to be sharpened before class.	9:42		X	
Looks like Jeff is ready to get started.	9:43	X		
Jack needs to stop talking and follow along.	9:45		X	
Louise is patiently waiting for us to begin.	9:46	X		
Guys, you need to get paper out and follow along.	9:47		X	
I see Martin is ready!	9:48	X		
I can't begin until everyone's attention is up here.	9:49		X	
Tony, take your hood off your head, please.	9:49		X	
We have wasted 10 minutes waiting for some of you to get ready.	9:50		X	
Leslie is ready to go.		X		
Bob and Jack, we are waiting for you to pay attention.			X	
Thanks Steve, I see you are ready.		X		
When you come to class prepared, we can begin on time.			X	X
Ratio of praise to correction: 5:9		Preventive prompts: 2		

Developed by Theresa L. Benfante, Behavior Interventionist at Central Alternative School, Cobb County School District (Georgia). Used with permission.

Understanding Data-Collection Techniques and Approaches

Another way the selective verbatim technique can be used is to categorize the teacher's responses as "praise," "correction," or "preventive prompts," followed by the time, as is shown in Tool 6 (page 31). The data in Tool 6 shed light not only on the teacher's statements, but also on the patterns and routines for the beginning of the class period.

Global scan/anecdotal focuses on events, actions, or words said by the teacher, students, or both. Data that are scripted can take many forms. To chronicle the events, only a blank sheet of paper, eyes, and ears are needed to capture the events of the class. Anecdotal notes can focus on events as they unfold by time or just by events. If you choose to chronicle the events by time as they unfold in the classroom, a simple table may be effective and efficient. Tool 7 presents a form that may be drawn in a few seconds during an observation and will keep the observer organized and efficient in the data-scripting process.

Tool 7   Global Scan: Scripting Data by Time

Angle: Wide

Focus: General focus—everything that occurs in the classroom; events are recorded by time

Teacher: Rejer Browne   **Observer:** Kate Blanca

Date of Observation: March 12, 2011   **Start Time:** 10:30   **End Time:** 10:45

Total Observation Time: 15 minutes   **Period of the Day:** Morning

Number of Students Present: 10   **Grade Level:** Junior

Class: Mathematics   **Topic of the Lesson:** Beginning of the class

Date of Postobservation Conference: March 13, 2011

Time	Events that Occurred	Notes
9:05	Teacher makes sure that students are seated and ready for the class	The organization of the class was done quickly and efficiently
9:06	Jane comes in late—the teacher invites her to take a seat	
9:07	Teacher makes sure all students are present	Not all students are paying attention; two girls in the back of the classroom are showing each other pictures
9:08	Teacher announces the topic of the lesson	

This tool was developed by Oksana Parylo, a doctoral student at the University of Georgia, Athens. Used with permission.

It is recommended to divide the table by minutes, although it does not mean that every row of the table should be filled in. Note that the third column allows the observer to write down any thoughts, ideas, or questions he or she may have.

A word of caution: it is understandable that an observer should use a watch to record the time during an observation. However, if the observer frequently keeps looking at his or her watch during an observation, it may send a wrong message to a teacher. One way to get around this situation is to place a watch (or a cell phone) on the desk so the observer may glean the time without making the teacher uncomfortable.

Anecdotal Data Sample—by Time

9:05	Teacher asked student (male, red shirt) to elaborate on the "yes" response. . . . How S. E. Hinton developed the symbol of the Siamese fighting fish.
9:06	Student: "at the end of the story . . . he sets the rumble fish free and then he dies . . . the characters fight like the rumble fish."
9:07	Teacher asked a general question: "Are there other examples throughout the book?" (several hands go up . . . teacher calls on student who is fidgeting with her backpack)

Anecdotal Data Sample—Series of Events, No Time

- ◆ Teacher was at the door when students entered the room.
- ◆ Students knew the routine: they went to their seats, pulled out books, notebooks, and the homework assignment due (the agenda on the blackboard cued students on what to do to get ready for the period).
- ◆ When the bell rang, a student turned on the overhead projector; teacher pointed to the math problem—students began working on solving the word problem.
- ◆ Teacher took attendance, spoke briefly with a student at her desk, and walked up and down the aisles collecting homework assignments.
- ◆ Teacher focused students on the word problem—asked for the properties of the word problem before asking for the solution.
- ◆ Student in the back of the room (arm in cast) gave the answer to the word problem—320 pounds of coffee beans.
- ◆ Teacher asked student in front of the room to write the formula she used to get a different answer (285 was her response).
- ◆ As the student wrote the formula, teacher asked questions of another student who had the same answer.
- ◆ Student at the board "talked through" her answer and the steps she took to derive the answer.
- ◆ The teacher enlisted other students for answers to questions.
- ◆ Teacher transitioned the class to a page in their books—modeled how to analyze the word problem—wrote numbers on the board, enlisted students with helping her with the computations.

The next open-ended data collection tool (Tool 8, page 34) is another way to landscape classroom observation notes.

Tool 8   Open-Ended Classroom Observation Form

Angle: Wide

Focus: General focus—everything that occurs in the classroom

Teacher: Lakesha Williams   **Observer:** Sr. Florence

Date of Observation: January 16, 2011   **Start Time:** 9:05   **End Time:** 9:15

Total Observation Time: 10 minutes   **Period of the Day:** Period 2

Number of Students Present: 15   **Grade Level:** 7

Class: Band   **Location:** Band Room

Objectives to Be Observed (If none specified, write, "general."): General

Times	Observations
9:05	Students moved quickly and efficiently once they had their instruments.
9:08	Warm-up. Students performed warm-up exercises together.
9:10	Sally was asked where her instrument (clarinet) was. Response: "I left it at home." Teacher reminded Sally that this was the third time this month. Sally became upset and was sent to the counselor.
9:15	Teacher returned to the lesson with the large group.
	Additional Observations

The next classroom observation form (Tool 9) is open-ended but includes key areas, such as learning objective, instructional strategies, seating arrangement, and so forth, to focus the observation. Obviously, in a 15–20 minute classroom observation, an observer would not be able to comment on all of these areas; however, the areas are important to focus attention during an informal classroom observation.

Checklists

A narrow data-collection method is the checklist approach, in which data are usually tallied at the end so that patterns can be inferred; however, checklist data can also be descriptive. A sample of checklist data is detailed in Tool 10 (page 36).

The checklist data—although easy to tally or look for patterns of occurrence of events (e.g., how many times students raised their hands or the number of questions asked)—can limit describing or giving specific detail about the events observed. One way to combat

Tool 9   Open-Ended—Key Areas

Angle: Wide

Focus: Selected key areas (e.g., learning objectives, instructional strategies, seating arrangement, and calling patterns)

Teacher: Jose Hernandez

Observer: Gregory Torchenski

Date of Observation: January 31, 2011

Start Time: 11:30   **End Time:** 11:40

Total Observation Time: 10 minutes

Period of the Day: 4th

Number of Students Present: 24

Grade Level: 9th (girls)

Class: Health

Topic of the Lesson: Weight Management/ Nutrition

Date of Postobservation Conference: February 1, 2011

I. Learning Objective: Appropriate eating and physical activities that support weight management (posted on white board and handout).

II. Instructional Strategies (also note time): 11:30–11:37 Lecture on calories and physical activity to burn calories. Had students stand and run in place for one minute. Led discussion on the amount of physical activity needed to maintain or lose weight.

III. Seating Arrangement:

IV. Transition Strategies: Cued students "stand and run briskly" and blew whistle to stop running in place.

V. Calling Patterns:

VI. Markers of Student Engagement: All students were engaged. The physical activity was a positive way to illustrate calorie burning.

this is to provide a space for a principal, supervisor, or coach to take observational notes, in addition to checking off the checklist items. Compare the observation form in Tool 11 (page 37) with the observation form in Tool 10 (page 36). The principal, supervisor, or coach is looking for the same data to be tallied but also records any important observational data related to the item that was noted on the checklist. For ease of comparison, the background information (i.e., teacher, observer, topics of the lesson) and checklist options are kept the same.

Tool 11 allows a principal, supervisor, or coach to note the time when certain teacher or student behavior occurred, which enables him or her to track the sequence of events that happened in a classroom during an observation. In addition, it allows a principal,

Text continues on page 38.

Data Collection

Tool 10   Sample Checklist Classroom Observation Form

Angle: Narrow

Focus: Teacher's actions and/or students' actions

Teacher: Nancy Chandley   **Observer:** Martine Orozco

Date of Observation: February 12, 2011   **Start Time:** 10:25   **End Time:** 10:45

Total Observation Time: 20 minutes   **Period of the Day:** Block 2

Number of Students Present: 26   **Grade Level:** Freshman

Class: English 1   **Topic of the Lesson:** Writing narrative essays

Date of Postobservation Conference: February 13, 2011

Students were:

- ☐ working in small, cooperative groups
- ☐ making a presentation
- ☐ taking a test
- ☑ working independently at their desks
- ☐ viewing a film
- ☐ other _____

Teacher was:

- ☐ lecturing
- ☐ facilitating a question-and-answer sequence
- ☑ working independently with students
- ☐ demonstrating a concept
- ☐ introducing a new concept
- ☐ reviewing for a test
- ☐ coming to closure
- ☐ other _____

Comments:

Nancy: Students were working independently at their desks. The arrangement of the room (desk, podium, table) allowed you to work independently with students on their essays and to keep an eye on students working at their desks.

Perhaps you should hold the next freshman-level meeting in your room so others can see your room arrangement.

Thanks for letting me visit your room and see the work you do to help our students become better writers. I appreciate your efforts.

—Martine Orozco

Tool 11   Extended Checklist Classroom Observation Form

Angle: Narrow

Focus: Teacher's actions and/or students' actions

Teacher: Nancy Chandley

Observer: Martine Orozco

Date of Observation: February 12, 2011

Start Time: 10:00   **End Time:** 10:20

Total Observation Time: 20 minutes

Period of the Day: Block 2

Number of Students Present: 26

Grade Level: Freshman

Class: English 1

Topic of the Lesson: Writing narrative essays

Date of Postobservation Conference: February 13, 2011

Check	Students were...	Time	Notes
X	Working in small, cooperative groups	10:00–10:10	
	Making a presentation		
	Taking a test		
X	Working independently at their desks	10:10–10:20	Some students chose to do this assignment in pairs, although they were instructed to work alone.
	Viewing a film		
	Other:		

Data Collection

supervisor, or coach to use the same table with checklist options for the whole duration of observation—the time option makes it clear that these events did not occur at the same time. It also allows the teacher and observer to compare what the teacher and students did at the same time during the lesson.

Tool 12 provides an example of a mixed-method informal classroom observation instrument.

Tool 12 Mixed-Method Informal Classroom Observations—Daves Creek Elementary School

Angle: Narrow

Focus: Learning environment (based on clearly defined criteria)

Teacher: *Stephanie Baker*   **Administrator:** *Roger Clarke*

Date of Observation: *March 17, 2011*   **Time:** *8:01 to 8:12*

Learning Environment

Presence = X	Criteria	Example Evidence
X	The classroom is neat/well organized; safety information is posted; Gotta Go Bag is accessible.	*Room was set up so students could move to different areas without incident.*
	Artifacts are standards/curriculum-based, level appropriate, and incorporate student work.	
	Essential questions relating to lesson posted in an area for students to see.	
X	Classroom rules clearly posted with rewards/consequences.	*Posted prominently on white board*
	Transitions are appropriate and smooth.	
X	Routines and procedures are in place and followed.	*Students knew how and where to put books and coats before going to seats.*
	Students show engagement to current lesson or task.	
	Mutual respect is evident.	

This tool was developed by Eric Ashton, principal, and Peggy Baggett, assistant principal, of Daves Creek Elementary School, and Kathy Carpenter, now principal at Riverwatch Middle School, in Forsyth County Public Schools (GA). Used with permission.

Presence = X	Criteria	Example Evidence
	Varied strategies and use of graphic organizers are used to meet needs of diverse learners— ESOL, EIP, special ed, and gifted.	
X	Student work is meaningful and has "real-life" application.	*Great anticipatory comments on the lesson "caring for others" by using pet analogies*
	Students are provided with specific and descriptive feedback throughout lesson to target areas of improvement.	
X	Varied levels of student work samples are posted for the purpose of student self-assessing against standards.	*Separate bulletin board for displaying student work*
X	Support for reading and math AIM goals is evident.	*There are many posters for reflecting goals.*
	Guided Reading Lessons: • Small-group reading purpose before and after • Running reading records • Genre • Graphic organizers • Questions/critical thinking	
	Variety of student grouping is used to meet individual student needs.	

Comments:

Stephanie, it was good to see how students respond to your expectations for the day, especially since this is the first day back from spring break.

---

*WOW is "Working on the Work," a reform construct developed by Phil Schlechty (*Shaking Up the Schoolhouse*, 2000).

The following checklist (Tool 13) was developed for supervisors and literacy coaches during informal and formal classroom observations.

The strength of the checklist method is its ease of use; the principal, supervisor, or coach takes in information and checks off what was observed or heard during the observation period. A weakness is that it is often difficult to reduce words or actions to a predetermined category on a checklist form.

Tool 13   Literacy Classroom Observation Checklist

Angle: Narrow

Focus: Literacy block; guided reading; literacy strategies

Teacher: Emily Watkins   **Observer:** Pat Dooley

Date of Observation: January 24, 2011   **Start Time:** 10:15   **End Time:** 10:30

Total Observation Time: 15 minutes   **Number of Students Present:** 18

Grade Level: 4th Grade   **Topic of the Lesson:** Word Recognition

Date of Postobservation Conference: January 25, 2011

Literacy Block	Guided Reading	Well Organized Classroom
☐ read aloud ☐ phonemic awareness (K-2) ☐ concepts of print (K-2) ☐ shared reading ☐ guided reading ☐ centers/independent work ☐ Monitored Independent Reading (MIR) ☒ explicit whole-class instruction ☒ word work ☒ phonics/spelling ☒ comprehension ☐ fluency ☐ oral language ☐ interactive/shared writing ☐ modeled writing ☐ directed writing ☐ 6+1 traits of writing ☐ writer's workshop ☐ independent writing	☐ small group area evident ☐ uses appropriate narrative texts ☐ uses appropriate informational texts ☐ differentiates instruction to meet all students' needs ☐ uses before, during, after activities ☐ incorporates comprehension ☐ incorporates fluency ☐ teaches vocabulary of text ☐ listens to students read ☐ conducts running records ☐ has up-to-date records ☐ uses appropriate reading strategies (whisper, staggered, choral, paired, etc.) NO ROUND-ROBIN reading!	☒ posts and uses rules, schedules, management system ☐ students routinely follow established rules and procedures ☒ smooth transitions ☐ room organized, labeled ☐ seating arranged for cooperative learning activities and interaction ☒ students accountable for learning ☒ room clutter free, inviting ☒ productive, workable noise level ☒ teacher has positive interaction with students ☒ positive interaction between students

Literacy Rich Classroom	Centers/Independent Work	Explicit Instruction
☐ print-rich environment	☐ management system in place	☒ grade-level teacher talk
☐ concept charts	☐ Students responsible for learning	☐ shared reading—all students
☒ definition charts	☐ engaging activities	☐ uses Houghton Mifflin for shared reading
☐ 6+1 Traits posters	☐ authentic reading/writing activities	☐ other grade-level texts (big books, poetry, informational); all students have access to text
☒ comprehension posters	☐ student accountability system	
☐ authentic reading/writing observed	☐ differentiated work matches student needs	☐ book talk
☐ student writing displayed	☐ work reinforces previously taught concepts	☐ preteaches vocabulary
☐ classroom library evident, with narrative & informational texts in a wide variety of genres, leveled appropriately, for student use		☒ uses comprehension strategies before, during, after activities
		☐ interactive, hands-on activities
		☐ integrated content core
☐ leveled book boxes for MIR		☐ incorporates good ESL strategies
☒ Word Wall posted, consisting of general and content words		

Writing	MIR	Word Work
☐ writing process	☐ minimum 15–20 minutes per day	☐ phonemic awareness (K-2)
☐ mini lesson		☐ phonics
☐ 6+1 traits of writing	☐ students self-select books from independent reading level; interest based books provided by teacher	☒ vocabulary
☐ student accountability/status of class		☒ differentiated spelling
☐ interactive/shared writing (K-2)	☐ variety of genres provided	☒ grade-level Language Arts
☐ modeled writing	☐ monitoring, nongraded (student reflections, cooperative learning discussions, conferences, bookmarks, journals, pictures, etc.)	☒ Word Wall posted
☐ directed writing		☒ Word Wall systematically used in instruction
☐ independent writing		
☐ student published writing available to other students		
☐ writing area & materials evident		

Assessment	Collaboration	Curriculum Mapping
☒ keeps up-to-date running records with guided reading levels	☐ collaborates with team in analyzing assessment data	☐ creates curriculum map based on Utah State Core and student needs
☐ submits guided reading levels as requested	☐ collaboratively plans for/ provides interventions, reteaching, enrichment, differentiation	☐ uses curriculum map to guide instruction
☒ maintains detailed formal and informal assessment records		
☐ maintains list of below level students		

This tool was developed by the Jordan School District, Sandy, UT. Acknowledgement is given to Dana L. Bickmore, former executive director for curriculum and staff development, and Kathy Ridd, elementary language arts and early childhood consultant of the Jordan School District. Used with permission.

Data Collection

Mixed-Method Data-Collection Techniques

Combining scripted (anecdotal) and checklist methods provides both qualitative and quantitative data about what was observed. Tool 14 offers a sample of how both open-ended (scripted) and narrow (checklist) data can be combined to chronicle the events of the classroom.

Tool 15 presents an open-ended form for collecting data in a foreign language classroom.

Tool 14 Anecdotal and Checklist Data-Collection Method: Focus on Cooperative Learning

Angle: Narrow

Focus: One or more aspects of cooperative learning (e.g., objectives, clarity of directions, and follow-up instructions)

Teacher: Janie Adams

Date of Observation: April 25, 2011

Total Observation Time: 20 minutes

Number of Students Present: 26

Class: US Gov.

Observer: Antonio Tanuta

Start Time: 9:05   **End Time:** 9:25

Period of the Day: Morning

Grade Level: Junior

Topic of the Lesson: Examining how a bill is passed

Date of Postobservation Conference: April 28, 2011

Focus	Presence = X	Notes
Objectives for the cooperative learning group	X	• Objective for the activity was written on the whiteboard. • Teacher referred to the objective as students asked questions. • Teacher returned to the objective during closure of group activity.
Clarity of directions	X	• Before breaking students into groups, teacher gave directions. • Teacher distributed directions for each group once students moved into their groups.
Movement into groups	X	• Six minutes for students to move into groups. • Materials were bundled for each group in advance.
Monitoring and intervening strategies	X	• Teacher turned lights on and off to get attention. • Teacher broke into group time three times with clarifying questions. • Teacher visited each group four times.
Interaction with students	X	• Asked questions and gave feedback to groups while monitoring. • Became a member of each group.
Follow-up instruction	X	• After 19 minutes, teacher called end to group work. • Students moved desks and chairs back in order.

Tool 15   Foreign Language Observation Checklist

Angle: Narrow

Focus: One or more aspects of foreign language teaching and learning (e.g., language modalities, culture, and learning materials)

Teacher: Marianna Smith   **Observer:** Johann Frederickson

Date of Observation: April 10, 2011   **Start Time:** 12:30   **End Time:** 12:50

Total Observation Time: 20 minutes   **Period of the Day:** 4

Number of Students Present: 28   **Grade Level:** 9 & 10

Class: French 2   **Topic of the Lesson:** French teenagers

Date of Postobservation Conference: April 11, 2011

1. **Are all language modalities evident in the lesson (speaking, writing, listening, and reading)?**
   Students heard a passage read by the teacher, then spoke with a partner or in a group of three to collectively summarize (in writing) the gist of the reading.

2. **Is culture evident in the lesson?**
   Because the passage was about French teens, culture was evident.

3. **Does the teacher use a wide variety of prepared and authentic materials at appropriate levels?**
   The reading was taken from an authentic French source—a Parisian teen magazine. Students were able to recreate the gist, so the level was apparently suitable for these learners.

4. **Is the purpose of each activity clearly explained to the students?**
   The activity had already begun when I entered. However, students seemed to have a clear understanding of what they were doing.

5. **Does the teacher model activities when giving directions and check for comprehension afterward?**
   Marianna gave directions before and after each of the two times she read the passage.
   When students had finished rewriting the passage summaries, three groups shared their summaries aloud with the class, and class members commented on the accuracy of information, making suggestions to augment, improve, and/or clarify the content of each.
   Marianna validated the information given, praised the students for their good work, and made suggestions for improvement.

6. **Are the transitions between activities smooth?**
   I only observed the passage summary activity.
   The class was preparing to move to a new activity when I left the room.
   The steps in the summary activity went smoothly from one to the next.

7. **Are the students on task and actively involved in the learning process?**
   Most students worked cooperatively with their partners.
   I noticed that there were three groups of three. In two of those groups, one student appeared to be much less involved than the other two students in the grouping.
   Because only one student was writing per group, I suggest breaking up the groups of three and sticking to pairs for this particular activity so that as many students as possible are highly engaged in the process.

8. **Is there an appropriate use of partner–pair or small group activities?**
   Yes, students worked in pairs (or groups of three as described above) with some brief moments of teacher-centered talk for the reading, directions, and feedback.

Developed by Marcia Wilbur, Ph.D., executive director, Curriculum and Content Development for the Advanced Placement Programs at the College Board, based on her work at Gull Lake High School Department, Richland, Michigan. Used with permission.

Data Collection

The Seating Chart

An efficient way to collect data is to use the seating chart. Generic seating charts can be made in advance, or teachers can be asked to provide a general seating chart of their rooms at the beginning of the year. Several techniques for observing student and teacher behaviors make good use of the seating chart to collect data. Advantages for using the seating chart to chronicle data include:

- ♦ *Ease of use.* A seating chart can be drawn within half a minute of entering the room.

- ♦ *Amount of data.* A large amount of information can be recorded on a single chart. (Consider breaking up the observation into five-minute increments—it is easy to get five minutes' worth of data on a single seating chart).

- ♦ *Focus on the events.* Important aspects of student behavior can be recorded while observing the teacher and the class as a whole.

If using the seating chart, it makes sense to have 15–20 copies available. The following generic seating chart (Tool 16) will assist you in collecting data. The observer can quickly sketch a seating chart upon entering the classroom.

Tool 16   Sample Seating Chart

Angle: Narrow

Focus: Events; teacher questions; student responses

Teacher: Marianna Smith   **Observer:** Johann Frederickson

Date of Observation: April 10, 2011   **Start Time:** 12:30   **End Time:** 12:50

Total Observation Time: 20 minutes   **Period of the Day:** 4

Number of Students Present: 28   **Grade Level:** 9 & 10

Class: French 2   **Topic of the Lesson:** French teenagers

Date of Postobservation Conference: April 11, 2011

Some examples of data that can be recorded easily on a seating chart include student–teacher question patterns, reinforcement and feedback, and classroom movement patterns. Using the seating chart to track question patterns can provide data on whether the teacher focuses only on a few students on one side of the room. The seating chart can also be used to track classroom movement patterns to determine whether the teacher lectures from the front of the room only or the types and frequency of feedback and reinforcement given to students. The same seating chart can be used to track several actions by supervisors comfortable focusing on more than one activity during the classroom observation. With a clear set of symbols, a principal, supervisor, or coach can track teacher movement patterns, student question patterns, teacher question pattern, or feedback. Examine Tool 17 (page 46) for more information.

The form has a field to note the time of the specific observation moment (e.g., 12:20–12:25; 12:25–12:30). This helps the principal, supervisor, or coach arrange the seating charts in chronological order. From the classroom movement pattern, we can see that the teacher did not come to Students 7 and 8, but the teacher walked to the desks of all other students in the room. From the question patterns, we notice that Student 1 was most frequently asked the questions and responded correctly to all of them; Students 3, 5, and 6 were asked one question each; and again, Students 7 and 8 were ignored. Of course, the data collected over the period of five minutes do not allow the observer to make any conclusions. Only in comparison with the other seating charts from the same observation and those from other days could the teacher and observer see if Students 7 and 8 did not get as much of the teacher's attention as other students in the class.

Now, compare the two seating charts presented in the Tool 16 and Tool 17. The seating chart in Tool 16 is pretty simple and shows only students' seats, the teacher's desk, and a file cabinet. Conversely, the seating chart in the Tool 17 is more elaborate and notes the desk of the observer and the entrance door and numbers the students for easy reference. Both types of seating charts can be effectively used, and the choice of one over the other depends on the objective for the classroom observation. The symbols used in Tool 17 are given for reference only; the observer should develop a list of symbols that are meaningful for him or her while denoting a certain action to be observed.

Use Technology to Assist with Tracking Classroom Observation Data

Advances in technology can enhance the collection of data during classroom observations. Observers can enter data on a handheld device, import the data to a laptop, and print the data collected during a classroom observation. Follow-up notes can be communicated prior to the postobservation conference using e-mail.

With the prevalence of the laptop computer with built-in and external recording device capabilities, observers can use the laptop not only to take notes during observations, but also to audio- or videotape teaching. When tools are combined with the features offered by computer database and spreadsheet applications, a rich rendition of teaching can be captured.

Future advances in technology will help principals, supervisors, and coaches capture the events of the classroom more reliably. However, there are a few caveats to consider when using technology to capture the events of the classroom. First, the availability of technology might be limited, and the observer might need to find funding sources to purchase a laptop, video camera, and other software applications. Second, at first,

Tool 17   Extended Seating Chart

Angle: Narrow

Focus: One or more aspects of classroom activities (e.g., questions, culture, and learning materials)

Teacher: Nancy Monterey   **Observer:** May Lee

Date of Observation: February 12, 2011   **Start Time:** 12:20   **End Time:** 12:25

Total Observation Time: 20 minutes   **Period of the Day:** Block 2

Number of Students Present: 8   **Grade Level:** Freshman

Class: English 1   **Topic of the Lesson:** The use of the semicolon

Observation Foci: teacher classroom movement pattern; teacher question pattern

Observation Legend:

The arrow is used to show the direction of the teacher's movement in a classroom.

?   denotes a question that a teacher asked a student, noted inside the box that represents a student.

?+   denotes that a student answered the question.

?−   shows that the student did not answer the question.

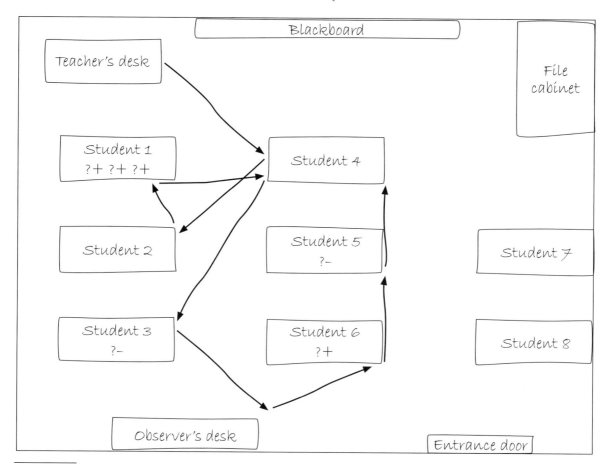

This tool was developed by Oksana Parylo, a doctoral student at the University of Georgia, Athens. Used with permission.

teachers might not want to be videotaped, so it is best to ask before taping. There might also be union considerations to consider. In some systems, classroom observers can only observe without taking notes. Third, some systems strictly forbid students from being videotaped without written permission of parents. Fourth, observers would need to be trained to use technology and have the opportunity to practice the skills needed to use technology to support classroom observations.

Whichever method of data collection is chosen, it is a good idea to detail major events, such as teacher questions and student responses. A few strong examples with complete and accurate information will make more sense for both the teacher and supervisor than will a long record of unfiltered information.

Looking Ahead...

Chapter 4 explores data-collection tools that the principal, supervisor, and coach can use while stepping out to observe teachers.

Data Collection

4

Looking in
While Stepping Out

In This Chapter...

♦ Supervisors and coaches use data collection tools and their applications.

♦ Supervisors and coaches capture the events of the classroom using a variety of observation tools.

This chapter includes tools designed to help supervisors and coaches emerge as leaders while conducting informal classroom observations. The following tools are offered:

Teachers want the facts; they need to be able to examine and reflect on what these data mean during follow-up conversations with the principal, supervisor, or coach (see Chapter 5). To collect these data, observers need to use tools that will assist them in focusing on specific aspects of teaching, student engagement, and the myriad activities that occur during the classroom period. This chapter describes tools that enable observers to collect data more reliably. Understanding and applying the tools of data collection, observers have firm footing to conduct informal observations that can help teachers focus on their classroom practices.

Data-Collection Tools and Their Application

Several tools are available and detailed here that will help principals, supervisors, or coaches track data from informal classroom observations. Unless otherwise indicated, the tools in this section are modified from the second edition of this book. To illustrate these applications, each description includes the following:

- ◆ background

- ◆ observation focus

- ◆ observation technique

- ◆ explanation of the tool and technique

- ◆ how and why the technique is helpful

- ◆ directions and approaches for using the tool

♦ where appropriate, alternative data-collection techniques and tools to extend data collection

♦ tips for using the technique

♦ suggested postobservation conference strategies

The following data-collection tools can help you track data from classroom observations. Principals, supervisors, and coaches are encouraged to use their imaginations and revise these forms to develop unique renditions appropriate to the particular classroom contexts in their schools: subject areas, grade levels, and the personnel teaching (e.g., teacher and paraprofessional, regular and special education coteaching partners). As a reminder, there are two decisions that are made when entering a classroom for an informal classroom observation:

1. where to focus the observation, based on what is occurring in the classroom

2. what data-collection tool or strategy to use to capture a rich portrayal of the events of the classroom

Given that this book is promoting informal classroom observations, the school leaders, coaches, and others conducting informal observations who are out and about will be likely to conduct several informal classroom observations a day; therefore, tracking critical information about each observation is important. For each informal classroom observation, the following information should be noted in addition to the data collected during the observation:

♦ teacher name

♦ observer name

♦ date of the observation

♦ period of the day

♦ title of class

♦ grade level

♦ beginning time of the observation

♦ ending time of the observation

♦ total time spent in observation

♦ number of students present

♦ topic of the lesson

♦ purpose of the observation

♦ focus of this classroom observation

♦ observation tool that was used

♦ date of postobservation conference

This information is helpful when following up with the observed teacher and tracking which teachers are being observed and when. As a time-management strategy, this information helps a school leader determine the time of day observations are occurring. For example, at the end of a month, an observer is able to determine whether more informal classroom observations were conducted in the morning or the afternoon or whether the observations were evenly distributed throughout the day. Moreover, such a tracking system ensures that all teachers benefit from informal classroom observations. Additionally, noting the purpose and focus of the observation, as well as the observation tool used, helps the observer quickly refresh his or her memory of the observation and the classroom. It will also allow the observer to quickly compare the foci of the classroom observations that he or she conducted and will help in planning future classroom observations.

Observation Guide Using Bloom's Taxonomy: Call and Response Background

Teachers spend much time talking with students—lecturing, giving directions, and asking and answering questions. To ensure understanding and application of knowledge, teachers commonly engage students in question-and-answer sessions, also referred to as call and response or Q&A. Questions can prompt responses ranging from simple recall of information to abstract processes of applying, synthesizing, and evaluating information. Bloom (1956) and his colleagues developed a continuum for categorizing questions and responses. Bloom's Taxonomy includes the following elements, arranged from lowest to highest order:

- *Knowledge.* Recalling specific facts

- *Comprehension.* Describing in one's own words

- *Application.* Applying information to produce some result

- *Analysis.* Subdividing something to show how it is put together

- *Synthesis.* Creating a unique, original product

- *Evaluation.* Making value decisions about issues

Bloom's Taxonomy frames the analysis of both written and oral questions. Figure 4.1 (page 52) provides an overview of Bloom's Taxonomy of questioning. Note that the continuum represents lower-order to higher-order thinking. Asking the right question is more important than getting the right answer. By focusing on questioning and answering segments during a lesson, the classroom observer will be able to help the teacher analyze not only the questions, but also the types of responses. By reviewing classroom observation notes, the teacher can examine student responses (e.g., higher-order questions with higher-order responses or, the converse, lower-order questions with lower-order responses). Moreover, the teacher will be able to assess student understanding and mastery and areas that might need to be retaught.

Framing questions that are challenging, open-ended, and uncluttered with extraneous information supports higher-order thinking (Abrami et al., 2008; Wang & Ong, 2003), and this is why examining both the teacher's questions and student responses to these questions is important. Three classroom observation tools (Tool 18, page 54; Tool 19, page 56; and Tool 20, page 57) offer the classroom observer assistance in tracking questions and student responses.

Bloom s Taxonomy and Definition	Sample Verb Stems	Students' Responses Would Indicate Skills Such As
Lowest Order		
Knowledge/Recall: Students are asked to remember information.	summarize, describe, interpret	memorizing, recognizing, identifying, and recalling
Comprehension: Students demonstrate they have understanding to organize and arrange material.	classify, discuss, explain, identify, indicate, locate, report, restate, review, translate	interpreting, translating from one medium to another, describing in one's own words, and organizing and selecting facts and ideas
Application: Students apply previously learned information to reach an answer to a different but similar problem.	apply, choose, demonstrate, dramatize, employ, illustrate, interpret, operate, practice, schedule, sketch, solve	solving problems and applying information to produce an end product
Analysis: Students critically examine events and perform certain operations, such as separating whole to part or part to whole.	analyze, calculate, categorize, compare, contrast, criticize, differentiate, discriminate, examine, question	subdividing, finding, identifying, and separating a whole into parts
Synthesis: Students produce an original work, make predictions, and/or solve problems.	arrange, create, assemble, design, compose, develop, construct, formulate, manage, organize, plan, prepare, propose	creating an original production
Highest Order		
Evaluation: Students answer a question that does not have an absolute answer, provide an educated guess about the solution to a problem, or render a judgment or opinion with backup support.	appraise, argue, assess, attach, defend, judge, rate, support, value, evaluate	making a decision, prioritizing information, and drawing a conclusion

Observation Guide Using Bloom's Taxonomy

Background

Observation Focus: questioning strategies based on the class discussion; the wording of questions; teacher questions; student questions

Observation Technique: selective verbatim

Explanation of the Tool and Technique: Selective verbatim is a word-for-word scripting of what was said by the person being observed. This tool is used to obtain complete information about the ways the questions or comments are used by the teacher or students. Selective verbatim is a narrow-lens tool that allows the observer to focus on select words of the teacher, the students, or both.

How and Why the Technique Is Helpful: This technique gives teachers feedback about the types of questions and the frequency of the types of questions asked. This technique can assist the teacher in examining the levels of understanding and comprehension of content based on student responses. This technique can also shed light on the proportion of higher- and lower-order questions asked over a specified time or on a specific topic being covered.

Directions and Approaches for Using the Tool: Using Tool 18 (page 54), the observer records only the questions the teacher asks of students. Write the sentence in the left-hand column. Put a check in the box that best describes the cognitive level of the question. (This may be part of the postobservation conference.)

Suggested Postobservation Conference Strategies: Tool 18

To promote engagement in the postobservation conference, Mr. Taylor brought the form to the conference with only the verbatim questions listed. Mr. Taylor encouraged Ms. Rodriguez to:

- Identify the level of thinking for each question noted, and then place a check mark in the grid (e.g., knowledge, comprehension, application, analysis, synthesis, or evaluation).

- Tally the number of questions at each level.

- Rework a few of the lower-order questions into higher-order questions.

Throughout the last step, Mr. Taylor asked probing questions: "What did you eventually want students to be able to do with the information being taught?" "How did the examples presented along with the questions help students understand the materials?" "Are there any clusters of questions that could have been extended beyond the knowledge level?"

Mr. Taylor relied on the data to lead the discussion. He let Ms. Rodriguez analyze the data, reflect on what the data meant for student learning, and rework questions that she had asked. Viewed within the framework of Bloom's Taxonomy, these questions enabled Ms. Rodriguez to reconstruct her instruction in terms of her focus—levels of questions.

During the last minutes of the postobservation conference, Mr. Taylor and Ms. Rodriguez targeted a few strategies to try before the next classroom observation. Of the ideas discussed, Ms. Rodriguez chose the following two:

1. Have a colleague videotape a lesson that includes a question-and-answer segment. Watching the video, document the questions he or she asked. Analyze the cognitive level of student responses, and identify any patterns in what was asked of the students.

2. Use a professional release day to observe a colleague teaching at another school in the district.

Tool 18   Observation Guide Using Bloom's Taxonomy

Angle: Narrow

Focus: Questioning strategies based on the class discussion

Teacher: Anita Rodriguez   **Observer:** Frank Taylor

Date of Observation: April 2, 2011   **Start Time:** 10:10   **End Time:** 10:30

Total Observation Time: 20 minutes   **Period of the Day:** Morning Block

Number of Students Present: 17   **Grade Level:** 4th grade

Class: Mathematics   **Topic of the Lesson:** Decimals

Date of Postobservation Conference: April 3, 2011

Time	Questions and Activities	Knowledge	Comprehension	Application	Analysis	Synthesis	Evaluation
				Levels of Thinking			
10:10	How many have heard the word "decimal"?	X					
	What do you think decimals are?	X					
	How do you know?		X				
	Have you ever seen a decimal?	X					
	What do you think that means?	X					
	Why the decimal? Why that period?		X				
10:15	Decimal points do what?	X					
	What makes the cents, not the dollar?	X					
	Why is 99 cents not a dollar?		X				
10:25	How would you write $200?	X					
	What does "00" mean?	X					
	Is that where Desmond saw a decimal point?	X					
	What instrument ... temperature?	X					
	How many kinds of them? Name two.	X					
10:30	What is she looking for?	X					
	What is a normal temperature?	X					
	Have you seen your temperature written?	X					
	Why do you think you need to use a decimal point?		X				

Tips: Tool 18

♦ During the observation, write the question. Then, in the postobservation conference, have the teacher identify the level of thinking for each question noted.

♦ Prior to the postobservation conference, identify the level of thinking for each question and have the teacher do the same. Compare and analyze your notes during the postobservation conference.

♦ An alternative strategy is to ask the teacher to rework a lower-order question into a higher-level question. Go back and forth.

A word of caution: if the teacher knows that he or she is observed for a type and frequency of questions used, that teacher may try to use more higher-order questions than usual.

Another way to landscape data, using a more wide-angle lens, related to teacher questions and the level of questions, is presented in Tool 19 (page 56). During the post-observation conference, ask the teacher to identify the taxonomy level.

Tips : Tool 19

♦ During the observation, focus on scripting as many questions as you possibly can without analyzing the taxonomy level.

♦ Note the approximate time when the question was asked.

♦ During the postobservation conference, let the teacher decide on the taxonomy level of the questions asked, making his or her decisions based on the data.

Bloom's Taxonomy can also be used to track and analyze the questions asked by students. You can easily adapt Tool 18 and Tool 19 to record student questions instead of the teacher questions. Tool 20 (page 57) provides an example of the tool to track student questions.

The principal, supervisor, or coach can give a copy of the filled-in observation guide to a teacher prior to the postobservation conference or bring a copy directly to the conference. Let a teacher analyze the data; let him or her place all student questions on the levels of Bloom's Taxonomy. If the majority of the questions fall on the lower-order level, have the teacher come up with ideas on how to teach students using higher-order questions.

Tools 18–20 exemplify the basic way of using Bloom's Taxonomy to analyze teacher or student questions. These basic observation guides can be extended to include an additional observation focus that will provide extra information. Note that, in Tool 21 (page 58), only one extra piece of information is looked for: to whom did the teacher direct the questions—to the whole class or to an individual student? The observer only has to write one letter, C (for class) or I (for individual), that corresponds to every question.

Tool 19 Alternative Observation Guide Using Bloom's Taxonomy

Angle: Narrow

Focus: Questioning strategies based on the class discussion

Teacher: Anita Rodriguez

Observer: Frank Taylor

Date of Observation: April 2, 2011

Start Time: 10:10   **End Time:** 10:30

Total Observation Time: 20 minutes

Period of the Day: Morning Block

Number of Students Present: 17

Grade Level: 4th grade

Class: 4th grade

Topic of the Lesson: Decimals

Date of Postobservation Conference: April 3, 2011

Time	Teacher Questions	Taxonomy Level
8:10	How many have heard the word "decimal"?	
	What do you think decimals are?	
	How do you know?	
	Have you ever seen a decimal?	
	What do you think that means?	
	Why the decimal? Why that period?	
10:15	Decimal points do what?	
	What makes the cents, not the dollar?	
	Why is 99 cents not a dollar?	
10:25	How would you write $200?	
	What does "00" mean?	
	Is that where Desmond saw a decimal point?	
	What instrument … temperature?	
	How many kinds of them? Name two.	
10:30	What is she looking for?	
	What is a normal temperature?	
	Have you seen your temperature written?	
	Why do you think you need to use a decimal point?	

Tool 20   Using Bloom's Taxonomy to Analyze Student Questions

Angle: Narrow

Focus: Student questions

Teacher: Janet Mendoza

Observer: Juan Rodrigues

Date of Observation: April 2, 2011

Start Time: 9:05   **End Time:** 9:20

Total Observation Time: 15 minutes

Period of the Day: Morning

Number of Students Present: 20

Grade Level: 4th grade

Class: Mathematics

Topic of the Lesson: Decimals

Date of Postobservation Conference: April 2, 2011, after school

Time	Student Questions	Taxonomy Level
9:05	1. What is a decimal? 2. Why is 99 cents not a dollar?	
9:10	1. What does "00" mean? 2. How do we write $250?	
9:15	1. What is the normal temperature? 2. Why do we need to know about decimals?	
9:20	1. Why do we write the temperature in decimals? 2. Where do we use decimals in everyday life?	

Tips: Tool 21

- ◆ You can use this form to see if the teacher addresses the questions to male and female students equally (use M and F accordingly).

- ◆ You can use an extra field to check if the question was answered or not (use yes or no or a simple check mark).

- ◆ You can use a field to note if the questions asked are simple (yes/no questions) or those that require full responses (how, why, what, etc).

- ◆ Remember—the possibilities are endless, and you can adapt these tools to serve all your observation needs within your particular school and district.

Tool 21 Extended Observation Guide Using Bloom's Taxonomy

Angle: Narrow

Focus: One or more aspects of classroom focusing on teacher questions

Teacher: Barty Crowford   **Observer:** Joseph Rower

Date of Observation: May 1, 2011   **Start Time:** 9:05   **End Time:** 9:20

Total Observation Time: 15 minutes   **Period of the Day:** Morning

Number of Students Present: 12   **Grade Level:** 4

Class: Mathematics   **Topic of the Lesson:** Decimals

Date of Postobservation Conference: May 2, 2011

Time	Teacher Questions	Directed to: Class (C) Individual (I)	Taxonomy Level
9:05	1. How many have heard the word "decimal"? 2. How do you know?	C I	Knowledge Analysis
9:10	1. Decimals point to what? 2. What do you think that means?	C C	Knowledge
9:15	1. What does "00" mean? 2. How would you write $200?	I C	
9:20	1. What is she looking for? 2. What is the normal temperature?	C C	

This tool was developed by Oksana Parylo, a doctoral student at the University of Georgia, Athens. Used with permission.

Focus on Wait Time

Background

A staple in teaching is the lecture and discussion in which student response carries the rate and pace of the experience. Teachers, noticing cues from students, make adjustments in the pace and pitch of the classroom discussion. At the heart of lecture, discussion, and group processing of knowledge is the asking of questions. How a teacher responds to questions is important for two reasons: the quality of response is related to wait time and the quality of the answer is related to wait time. Stahl (1994) related that, when students are given three seconds or more of undisturbed wait time, there are certain positive outcomes:

♦ The length and correctness of their responses increase.

♦ The number of "I don't know" and no-answer responses decreases.

- The number of volunteered, appropriate answers by larger numbers of students greatly increases.

- Students' scores on academic achievement tests tend to increase.

- When teachers wait patiently, in silence, for three seconds or more at appropriate places, positive changes in their own teacher behaviors also occur.

- Teachers' questioning strategies tend to be more varied and flexible.

- Teachers decrease the quantity and increase the quality and variety of their questions.

- Teachers ask additional questions that require more complex information processing and higher-level thinking on the part of students. (pp. 3–5)

Tool 22   Focus on Wait Time

Angle: Narrow

Focus: Wait time during class discussion or lecture

Teacher: Haidong Chen   **Observer:** Francesca Duncan

Date of Observation: April 18, 2011   **Start Time:** 8:05   **End Time:** 8:20

Total Observation Time: 15 minutes   **Period of the Day:** Period 1

Number of Students Present: 24   **Grade Level:** Grade 9

Class: English I   **Topic of the Lesson:** S. E. Hinton's Rumble Fish

Date of Postobservation Conference: April 21, 2011

Teacher Questions	Wait Time (Seconds)
…in what year?…James?	2 seconds
When you think of the lessons the characters learned by the end of the book, who do you think grew up the most?	3 seconds
How does the Siamese fighting fish come to be symbolic of the characters in this book?	5 seconds
Leslie, are there any other symbols?	4 seconds
Do these other symbols relate to the importance of the Siamese fighting fish?	2 seconds
Why do you suppose S. E. Hinton chose Siamese fighting fish, rather than another type of domestic fish?	6 seconds

Additionally, Egan, Cobb, and Anastasia (2009) reported that think time and wait time develops respect among students and teachers and extends beyond the classroom. From the research of Stahl (1994) and others (e.g., Egan, Cobb, & Anastasia, 2009; Rowe, 1986; Tobin, 1987), wait time is think time, and three seconds has been reported as the ideal amount of time to wait for student response.

Observation Focus: wait time during class discussion or lecture

Observation Technique: wide-angle approach that focuses not so much on the questions as on the wait time between when the teacher finishes the question and when a student is called on to answer the question

Explanation of the Tool and Technique: Once the teacher completes articulating the question, track the wait time afforded before calling on a student to answer the question.

How and Why the Technique Is Helpful: This tool can help the teacher to focus on the amount of wait time between the question and the response while examining the complexity of questions. This type of data can help the teacher and observer examine student engagement and understanding of concepts, as well as the pace of questions asked.

Directions and Approaches for Using the Tool: Using a watch with a second hand, note the time the teacher waits between completing the question and calling on a student. Note as much of the question as possible, focusing more on the end words of the question.

Tips: Tool 22

♦ Place your watch flat on the desk so that the teacher does not focus on you looking at the watch.

♦ Note as many questions as possible. It is more important to capture illustrative examples than every question the teacher asks.

Another way to track wait time is to landscape data by including the taxonomy level of the questions related to wait time. This type of data can enhance analysis and reflection by examining both the type of questions using Bloom's Taxonomy and the amount of wait time (see Tool 23).

Tips: Tool 23

♦ Suggest the teacher analyze wait time in terms of the type of question asked.

♦ Leave the "Question Domain" column blank and let the teacher fill in the level of taxonomy.

♦ If there is an overreliance on lower-level domains, role-play with the teacher to rephrase the questions to move toward higher-order domains.

Tool 23   Using Bloom's Taxonomy to Examine Levels of Questions

Angle: Narrow

Focus: Examining teacher questions and/or student questions

Teacher: Haidong Chen   **Observer:** Francesca Duncan

Date of Observation: April 18, 2011   **Start Time:** 8:05   **End Time:** 8:20

Total Observation Time: 15 minutes   **Period of the Day:** Period 1

Number of Students Present: 24   **Grade Level:** Grade 9

Class: English I   **Topic of the Lesson:** S. E. Hinton's Rumble Fish

Date of Postobservation Conference: April 21, 2011

Teacher Questions	Wait Time (Seconds)	Question Domain
...in what year?...James?	2 seconds	Knowledge
When you think of the lessons the characters learned by the end of the book, who do you think grew up the most?	3 seconds	Synthesis, Evaluation
How does the Siamese fighting fish come to be symbolic of the characters in this book?	5 seconds	Analysis
What deeper meanings can you apply to letting the fish out of their tanks at the end of the story?	3 seconds	Evaluation

Suggested Postobservation Conference Strategies: Tool 23

Ms. Duncan prepared for the postobservation conference by thinking about the wait time in relation to the types of questions Mr. Chen asked. During the postobservation conference, Ms. Duncan:

♦ invited Mr. Chen to review his questions and the amount of wait time he allowed

♦ suggested that Mr. Chen analyze wait time in terms of the type of question asked, using Bloom's Taxonomy

♦ encouraged Mr. Chen to determine if there were any other patterns to questions—more or less wait time during question groupings (e.g., Evaluation versus Knowledge)

For an experienced observer, this tool can be extended by examining extra data that are typically available. These extra data may include the gender of the student who was asked the question or the audience for a question—whether the question was asked to an individual group or to the whole class. Note how Tool 24 allows a principal, supervisor, or coach to focus on two aspects at the same time—whether the question was asked to an individual student or to the whole class and, if it was asked to an individual student, whether it was a male or female student. This piece of data will allow a teacher to compare the wait time he or she allows to individual and group questions.

Tool 24   Using Bloom's Taxonomy to Examine Levels of Questions (Extended)

Angle: Narrow

Focus: Examining teacher questions and/or student questions

Teacher: *Haidong Chen*   **Observer:** *Min Chen*

Date of Observation: *January 12, 2011*   **Start Time:** *9:00*   **End Time:** *9:15*

Total Observation Time: *15 minutes*   **Period of the Day:** *Period 1*

Number of Students Present: *20*   **Grade Level:** *Grade 9*

Class: *English I*   **Topic of the Lesson:** *S.E. Hinton's Rumble Fish*

Date of Postobservation Conference: *January 13, 2011*

Teacher Question	Directed to: Class (C) Male Student (M) Female Student (F)	Wait Time (Seconds)	Taxonomy Level
In what year?	*M*	*2 seconds*	*Knowledge*
When do you think of the lessons the characters learned by the end of the book, who do you think grew up the most?	*C*	*3 seconds*	*Synthesis, Evaluation*
How does the Siamese fighting fish come to be symbolic of the characters in this book?	*C*	*5 seconds*	*Analysis*
What deeper meanings can you apply to letting the fish out of their tanks at the end of the story?	*F*	*3 seconds*	*Evaluation*

This tool was developed by Oksana Parylo, a doctoral student at the University of Georgia, Athens. Used with permission.

Focus on Calling Patterns and Patterns of Interaction

Background

Teachers often wonder about their calling patterns. They want to know who they are calling on and how often, whether they call on everyone, and whether they favor any one group of students or an area of the classroom. The patterns of interaction between a teacher and students are an essential part of the teaching and learning process.

Observation Focus: calling and interaction patterns during a class period

Observation Technique: narrow lens

Explanation of the Tool and Technique: A narrow lens is used to track calling patterns—which students are engaging with the teacher. A seating chart is used to notate calling and interaction patterns.

How and Why the Technique Is Helpful: Teachers can use the information to determine if they are calling on a variety of students, if any students are not participating, and if certain individuals are dominating class time.

Directions and Approaches for Using the Tool: Note the calling patterns (i.e., entire class responding, individual response, individual assistance, and so on). Develop a code for each. During the observation, track calling patterns on a seating chart (Tool 25, page 64).

Tips: Tool 25

♦ Ask a teacher to provide you with the seating chart of a classroom ahead of time.

♦ Always have several copies of the seating chart if you are doing this type of observation.

♦ Develop your own legend, using the contracted words, but make it clear to the teacher what these contractions mean.

Suggested Postobservation Conference Strategies: Tool 25

The data recorded on the chart enables the teacher to review his or her own calling patterns (i.e., frequency, gender, and so forth). Lead the teacher through examining the calling patterns as portrayed in Tool 26 (page 65). This approach focuses broadly on the distribution of calling patterns across boys and girls.

Analysis: Tool 26

♦ 20 students in the classroom

♦ 7 female and 13 male

♦ 9 questions directed to females

♦ All 7 females were interacted with

♦ 9 students interacted with one time

Text continues on page 66.

Looking In

Tool 25   Tracking Calling Patterns

Angle: Narrow

Focus: Calling and interaction patterns during a class period

Teacher: Susan Petrulis   **Observer:** Francie Parker

Date of Observation: October 25, 2011   **Start Time:** 11:00   **End Time:** 11:20

Total Observation Time: 20 minutes   **Period of the Day:** 4th period

Number of Students Present: 20   **Grade Level:** 7th Grade

Class: Social Studies   **Topic of the Lesson:** Vietnam War

Date of Postobservation Conference: October 27, 2011 (after school)

Legend

Entire Class Response: ECR   Individual Response: IR

Individual Help: IH   Question: Q   Comment: C

Front of Room

	A	B	C	D
1	Charles	James 11:12–IR 11:16–IR 11:20–IR	Mary (sitting in back) 11:01–IR 11:05–Reading 11:12–IR	Sam 11:07–IR 11:10–Q 11:15–IH 11:18–IR
2	Christine 11:10–Q to teacher 11:14–IR (w/ repeat)	Tony 11:01–IR 11:02–C 11:10–IR	Andrea Absent	Randy 11:08–IR 11:09–Reading 11:20–IR
3	Michael	Tiffany 11:04–IR 11:06–C	Jean 11:00–C/R 11:11–IH 11:14–IR 11:18–C	Sandy
4	Patrick Suspended	Jeff Absent	Kristy 11:03–Q 11:05–IH 11:13–IR	Amber 11:14–C 11:17–Q 11:18–Q
5	Andrew 11:07–IR 11:09–Reading 11:14–IR	Tyson 11:04–C made by teacher 11:08–C 11:12–C	Kate Absent	

Tool 26 Tracking Calling Patterns—Seating Chart

Angle: Narrow

Focus: Calling and interaction patterns during a class period

The following approach focuses broadly on the distribution of calling patterns across boys and girls.

Teacher: *Susan Petrulis*   Observer: *Francie Parker*

Date of Observation: *October 27, 2011*   Start Time: *11:00*   End Time: *11:20*

Total Observation Time: *20 minutes*   Period of the Day: *4th period*

Number of Students Present: *20*   Grade Level: *7th Grade*

Class: *Social Studies*   Topic of the Lesson: *Vietnam War*

Date of Postobservation Conference: *October 27, 2011 (after school)*

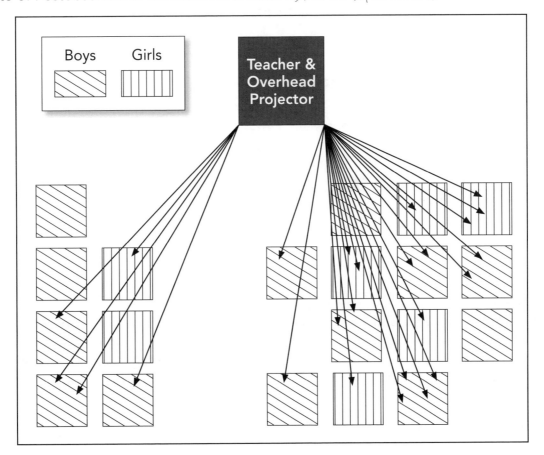

This tool was developed by Meredith A. Byrd, Clayton County Public Schools (Jonesboro, GA). Used with permission.

- ◆ 5 students interacted with two times

- ◆ 1 student interacted with three times

- ◆ 1 student interacted with four times

- ◆ 19.2% of teacher interaction was directed to the right side of the classroom, which consisted of 7 students

- ◆ 80.8% of teacher interaction was directed toward the left side of the classroom, which consisted of 13 students

Suggested Postobservation Conference Strategies: Tool 26

The patterns, as depicted in the analysis, will lead to follow-up questions. Teaching is full of blind spots, such as avoiding certain areas of the classroom, overcalling on certain students, such as those easily distracted, and, in some cases, calling on more boys than girls or girls than boys. The key is to help the teacher "see" the patterns that emerge in the data.

Cause and Effect

Background

Classrooms are highly interactive environments. Examining cause and effect can help teachers examine the effect that their words and actions have on students. This process works in reverse as well; the actions and words of students can have an effect on what teachers do and say.

Observation Focus: tracking teacher behaviors to determine the effects they have on students

Observation Technique: wide-angle lens technique that examines teacher's actions and words and the effects they have on students

Explanation of the Tool and Technique: This tool is designed to give the observer and the teacher information concerning the influence of the teacher's actions on students' responses in the classroom. This tool can be useful in observing a teacher's classroom management, direction giving, feedback giving, and other teacher behaviors related to student response.

How and Why the Technique Is Helpful: This type of information can be especially helpful for new teachers or teachers experiencing difficulties with classroom management (i.e., managing student behavior, learning activities, and transitions).

Directions and Approaches for Using the Tool: Divide a blank sheet of paper into two columns. Record teacher actions in the left-hand column, and record student responses to these actions in the right-hand column.

Tool 27 can be easily adapted to record how a teacher reacts to student actions. Note that Tool 28 (page 68) allows an observer to differentiate between the behavior of all students and the actions of individual students. It does not mean, however, that both fields for student behaviors should be filled in for all observation time. If a principal,

Tool 27 Cause and Effect

Angle: Narrow

Focus: Tracking teacher behaviors to determine the effects they have on students

Teacher: James Ackman   **Observer:** Juanita Powell

Date of Observation: May 5, 2011   **Start Time:** 1:15   **End Time:** 1:35

Total Observation Time: 20 minutes   **Period of the Day:** 6th period

Number of Students Present: 26   **Grade Level:** Mixed (Juniors and Seniors)

Class: Accounting I   **Topic of the Lesson:** Using Accounting Software

Date of Postobservation Conference: May 6, 2011

Time	Teacher	Student Response or Activity
Bell (1:15)	At desk organizing papers	Milling around room
1:15–1:21	Takes roll Makes announcements Collects homework	Quietly talking
1:22	Turns on overhead and says, "Take out your notebooks and open your book to page 140."	Students pull out materials. Red shirt slapping boy next to him (blue shirt).
1:23	"Folks, heads up to the overhead and focus on the chapter objectives." Begins stating the objectives for the chapter	Shuffling to get their books out and open to page 140. Seven students (out of 16) do not have books.
1:19–1:23	"Read from pages 140 to 145." Teacher sitting at desk getting software to boot up for a demonstration	Students without books: Two are talking with each other Two are sleeping Three are reading from nearby student's books
1:24	"Who would like to offer a summary, while I get the program loaded?"	Four students are still reading; three students (who did not have book) are talking with their neighbors; two students sleeping; four students raise their hands; one student asks a question out loud, "How can you expect us to finish reading five pages in 10 minutes," and another student blurts, "Bite me."
1:26	"James, repeat what you said."	James: "Bite me."
1:27	"James, I just cannot believe you said, 'bite me.' Are you talking to me?"	"Yeah, yeah, just 'get bit,' Ackman."
1:28	Pushes the call button for assistance	Eight students talking; three laughing, James walks to the door

Continued

Time	Teacher	Student Response or Activity
1:29	Loading computer program	Students are talking among themselves.
1:30	Announces: Technology is not cooperating today. Pull out books and look at the study questions at the end of the chapter	Students pull out books and start to thumb through the chapter.

Tool 28 Alternative Approach to Cause and Effect

Angle: Narrow

Focus: Tracking teacher behaviors to determine the effects they have on students

Teacher: James Ackman   **Observer:** Juanita Powell

Date of Observation: May 5, 2011   **Start Time:** 9:05   **End Time:** 9:20

Total Observation Time: 15 minutes   **Period of the Day:** 6th period

Number of Students Present: 26   **Grade Level:** Seniors

Class: Accounting 1   **Topic of the Lesson:** Using Accounting Software

Date of Postobservation Conference: May 6, 2011

Time	Student Behavior		Teacher Response
	Individual Students	**Students as a Class**	
9:05	Jack is drawing something; Jane and Jowell are giggling.	Quietly talking	Organizing the class to start the lesson
9:10	Lynn cannot find her book; Sam is showing something to a boy next to him.	Shuffling to get their books out	"Folks, heads up to the overhead and focus on the chapter objective."
9:15	Students without books: 2 are sleeping; 2 are talking with each other.	Most of the students are reading the pages as instructed.	"Read individually from page 140 to 145."
9:20	3 students are sleeping on their desks.	Talking among themselves	Loading computer program

This tool was developed by Oksana Parylo, a doctoral student at the University of Georgia, Athens. Used with permission.

supervisor, or coach observes an individual student's disruptive behavior, he or she can focus the whole observation on only that one (or several) student. The same is true if the principal, supervisor, or coach is interested in class dynamics and wants to observe students and their behavior and learning as a group.

Tips: Tools 28

♦ Record events in five-minute intervals.

♦ Record enough information for the teacher to make sense of the overall events of the classroom.

♦ Include verbal statements as necessary to focus conversation during follow-up with the teacher.

♦ Avoid making value judgments while chronicling what is observed.

♦ Focus on concrete actions, directions, or words of the teacher and the subsequent behavior of students.

Suggested Postobservation Conference Strategies: Tool 27 and Tool 28

Ask the teacher to examine the data. Ask probing questions related to the timing of events and how words led to escalating the events of the verbal exchange. Brainstorm with the teacher about other strategies that might have caused a different outcome. Topical areas could include the use of activities or strategies while the computer program was loading.

Variety of Instructional Methods

Background

Regardless of subject area, grade level, or the teacher's experience, a single class period should include a variety of instructional methods. Research has cast new light on the way children learn, and we can no longer assume that any one instructional strategy is sufficient to reach all learners all of the time. Effective teachers not only use a variety of instructional strategies, but also differentiate strategies. To differentiate, teachers provide alternative approaches to the methods used to present content and the ways that students show mastery of learning objectives. Given the myriad of ability levels of students and the recognition that no two learners learn at the same rate or in the same way, differentiated instruction shows great promise as a way of thinking about teaching and learning (Clark, 2010). In a classroom in which instruction is differentiated, students are offered a variety of ways to learn. According to Tomlinson (1999), differentiated instruction flourishes when the following occur:

♦ Teachers begin where the students are.

♦ Teachers engage students in instruction through different learning modalities.

♦ Students compete more against themselves than against others.

♦ Teachers provide specific ways for each individual to learn.

- Teachers use classroom time flexibly.

- Teachers are diagnosticians, prescribing the best possible instruction for each student. (p. 2)

Observation Focus: variety of instructional techniques

Observation Technique: narrow-angle lens technique focusing on the number of instructional strategies, the length of each, and the activities students engage in during each

Explanation of the Tool and Technique: For each instructional strategy used, indicate the time and what the teacher and the students are doing. Additional information, such as transitions, could also be noted. Tracking a variety of instructional strategies will require a longer classroom observation, perhaps an entire class period; however, it is not outside the realm of possibility for the principal, supervisor, or coach to observe in a classroom where more than one instructional technique is used in a 15–20 minute span of time.

How and Why the Technique Is Helpful: This technique can give insight about the number and duration of instructional strategies used during a class segment.

Tips: Tool 29

- Note teacher cues for each instructional method and the transitions between the methods or activities used to further the instruction.

- Note the length of each instructional method.

- If possible, have the teacher review observation notes prior to the postobservation conference.

Suggested Postobservation Conference Strategies: Tool 29

Later the same day, Julie Escobar visited Shelly Beter for a few minutes and asked her to review the observation notes so she could analyze the data on her own. The next day, Julie and Shelly met before school to discuss the classroom observation. Julie began the conversation with an open-ended question, "What patterns do you see?"

During the postobservation conference, Julie and Shelly reviewed the various instructional strategies used, the amount of time spent on each, what students were doing during each, and what learning objectives were being met. On reflection, Shelly shared that she really did not give students enough time to write out ideas and concepts on the note cards and that she would experiment with (1) extending the amount of time for note taking and (2) giving more explicit directions to students prior to having them work independently. She shared that some students were still having difficulties with finding "proofs" from the text of the novel.

Tool 29   Variety of Instructional Methods

Angle: Narrow

Focus: Instructional techniques; instructional materials used by the teacher

Teacher: Shelly Beter

Observer: Julie Escobar

Date of Observation: March 4, 2011

Start Time: 9:00   **End Time:** 9:25

Total Observation Time: 25 minutes

Period of the Day: Block 1

Number of Students Present: 25

Grade Level: 9th grade

Class: English I (Remedial)

Topic of the Lesson: S. E. Hinton's Rumble Fish

Date of Postobservation Conference: March 4, 2011

Time	Instructional Method	Teacher Behavior	Student Activities
9:00–9:05	Organizing lecture	Lecturing, Q & A period about plot Distributes an index card to each student: Directs students to write one sentence about the importance of the Siamese fighting fish	Listening, taking notes, asking questions
9:06–9:08	Independent work	Monitoring student work	Students write on the index cards
9:09–9:22	Large-group sharing	Teacher seeks volunteers to share insights about the Siamese fighting fish and its importance, thus far, in the book; asking for "proofs" from the text to support ideas written on the index cards Leading students to citations offered by groups	Sharing thoughts about the symbol of the Siamese fighting fish; finding citations from the text to support ideas
9:23–9:25	Question and answer	Asking questions	Responding to questions (looking up citations to back up ideas); asking questions

Examining Teacher-Student Discussion with a Focus on How Student Comments Are Incorporated into the Lesson

Background

Nothing keeps a class moving forward more than a lively discussion in which student responses are incorporated into the lesson. Teachers who incorporate student responses into lessons extend learning and are more readily able to check for understanding. Student responses also serve to assess student learning, giving cues to the connections students are making with content, their ability to apply what they are learning, and the areas that need to be reinforced or retaught. When a teacher incorporates student comments, such behavior signals a student-centered classroom in which student questions often serve to extend the concepts that are being studied.

Observation Focus: incorporating student comments and ideas into the discussion

Observation Technique: narrow focus using selective verbatim

Explanation of the Tool and Technique: This tool is designed to give the observer and the teacher information concerning how teachers incorporate student comments into class discussions.

How and Why the Technique Is Helpful: This technique can also help teachers assess student learning based on student responses and to become aware of the information student responses can give relative to understanding and application of concepts previously taught.

Directions and Approaches for Using the Tool: Note what the teacher says (focusing on questions), the student response to the question, and then what the teacher does with the student response.

Tip: Tool 30

♦ Given the fast nature of classroom discussions, writing question stems will suffice (e.g., "Can we find examples from the text...?").

Suggested Postobservation Conference Strategies: Tool 30

This data collection tool allows the observer to capture how the teacher incorporates student responses into the overall lecture and classroom discussion. Jeannette spends a few minutes having Jack look at what he did with student responses. To do this, Jeannette encouraged Jack to track the type of responses students gave and what he did to incorporate student responses into the discussion.

Jeannette then encouraged Jack to:

1. track what strategies he used, while incorporating comments

2. examine the types of questions he used to extend student thinking. Jack used Bloom's Taxonomy, and then he examined whether or not his questions were "open-ended," so that students could branch out into other related areas of the book

Tool 30 Examining Teacher-Student Discussion with a Focus on How Student Comments Are Incorporated into the Lesson

Angle: Narrow

Focus: Incorporating student comments and ideas into the discussion

Teacher: Jack Howard

Observer: Jeannette Geter

Date of Observation: April 28, 2011

Start Time: 8:50   **End Time:** 9:06

Total Observation Time: 16 minutes

Period of the Day: 2nd period

Number of Students Present: 25

Grade Level: 9th grade (Honors)

Class: English I

Topic of the Lesson: Symbolism found in S. E. Hinton's Rumble Fish

Date of Postobservation Conference: April 29, 2011

Time	Teacher Talk/Question	Student Responses	How Student Comments Are Used
8:50	A symbol is an object that represents something else. What are the symbols in Rumble Fish?	SR1: Siamese rumble fish SR2: The gangs are made up of people who can't get along with one another.	Can you expand on this? (Mr. Howard asks) Cite an example of this from the text.
8:53		SR3: See page 47.	Relate this to the end of the book
8:55		SR4: At the end, the Siamese fighting fish are let go.	Does this parallel the death of the character?
8:57	In your opinion, was letting the fish go an act of bravery?	SR5: He was making a statement about being free . . . on page 98 it says he was born in the wrong era.	OK, but was this act bravery or an act of cowardice?
9:01			What do you think the narrator meant by the "wrong era"?
		SR6: He just did not fit into the world he lives in.	What made him an outcast?
9:06	Can we find examples from the text that back up the idea he did not fit into the world he lives in?		

3. Jeannette asked Jack the following questions:

- ♦ Have students expanded on each other's ideas?

- ♦ Did students look up information in the book to support answers?

- ♦ Did students write their ideas in notebooks?

Focus on Tracking Transition Patterns

Background

The transition is, in a sense, an instructional method. Smooth transitions conserve time, help keep students focused on learning objectives, and lessen the opportunities for classroom disruptions. Transitions are enhanced when materials are assembled in advance, lessening the loss of time between activities and allowing smoother movement from one method of instruction to another. Transitions are seamless, with students assuming some responsibility for efficient operation. Transitions are more successful when teachers:

- ♦ establish and reinforce routines

- ♦ cue students to a transition, so they are ready to transition to the next activity

- ♦ provide clear directions as part of the transition

- ♦ have materials available before the transition begins

Observation Focus: transition strategies

Observation Technique: narrow angle, focusing only on the transitions that a teacher uses between activities or instructional segments

Explanation of the Tool and Technique: The principal, supervisor, or coach tracks which techniques the teacher uses between instructional segments—that is, how the teacher gets students from point A to point B.

How and Why the Technique Is Helpful: This technique helps the teacher examine how activities and instruction are organized and the amount of time it takes to move from one activity to another. For teachers who might be having difficulty with student behavior, this strategy can assist them in improving their classroom management.

Directions and Approaches for Using the Tool: Record broadly the instructional activity and then the transition (i.e., cues, clarity of directions) used to move students from one activity to another, focusing on student responses based on the transition strategy.

Suggested Postobservation Conference Strategies: Tool 31

Encourage the teacher to examine the transitions and how students respond throughout the transition periods. Suggest that the teacher examine the minutes involved in the transition, the directions or cues, and how students respond to these directions and cues.

Tool 31   Focus on Tracking Transition Patterns

Angle: Narrow

Focus: Transition strategies during instruction and classroom activities

Teacher: Cheryl Hofer

Observer: June Kaufman

Date of Observation: January 18, 2011

Start Time: 10:10   **End Time:** 10:24

Total Observation Time: 14 minutes

Period of the Day: Morning

Number of Students Present: 18

Grade Level: 4th grade

Class: 3rd grade (Math)

Topic of the Lesson: Map activity— geography

Date of Postobservation Conference: January 22, 2011

Instruction/Activity	Transition	Student Response
10:10–10:14: Getting students into cooperative groups	Gives directions for small cooperative group. Stops movement to give clarifying instructions. Hands out worksheets, maps, and other supplies.	Students meander, finding their group members; four students ask clarifying questions during movement.
	Teacher directs team captains to pick up direction sheet for their groups.	
	Materials are packaged on teacher's desk; packets have a number on them corresponding to the group (e.g., 1, 2, 3). Captains pick up packet.	Two groups did not know who the designated captain was.
10:15–10:24: Students are working in groups. Teacher is walking from group to group redirecting students, answering questions.		
10:20: Teacher reminds students that they have four minutes left to complete task.	Students continue to work; one group has completed the map— members are checking accuracy of sign markers.	
10:24: Getting students back into large group	Flicks lights on and off, asks Group 1 to send their rep to the front of the room to give a summary.	Students are moving desks back into rows and getting ready for whole-class work.

Tracking Student Behavior

Background

Tracking student behavior helps teachers experiencing classroom management issues, regardless of the teacher's experience level. However, observing student behavior is not necessarily related to discipline issues. Teachers establish classroom routines, plan lessons, organize materials, and interact with students with the best of intentions. Teachers can benefit from data about student behavior to pinpoint areas to be more aware of as they manage instruction, learning objectives, activities, and interactions with students. Data that clearly focus on student behavior and classroom- and instructional-management techniques can yield a fuller understanding of the complexities of teaching.

Observation Focus: student behavior

Observation Technique: narrow focus, broadly applied to tracking student behavior during instruction—directions, verbal and nonverbal cues from the teacher and student response

Explanation of the Tool and Technique: This tool will help the observer to focus on teacher behaviors and their effect on student behavior and response.

How and Why the Technique Is Helpful: With the fast-paced nature of instruction, sometimes teachers cannot readily analyze the effect their words have on student behavior. This tool can help the teacher analyze what is said and how students respond to what is being said, in addition to overall classroom management.

Directions and Approaches for Using the Tool: Track teacher behavior (i.e., words, routines, activities, directions), and then immediately note student behavior.

Tips: Tool 32

♦ Encourage the teacher to look for patterns in student behaviors.

♦ If needed, focus on one or several students whose behavior differs from the class (i.e., too disruptive, silent, active).

Suggested Postobservation Conference Strategies: Tool 32

Martin leaves his observation notes with Samuel so he can examine the data. When Martin and Sam meet the next day, Martin opens the discussion with the question, "How do you think things went in class yesterday with this group of students?" There is a long pause, and Samuel admits he needs help with this group of students. Martin agrees, and he thinks the best way to proceed is to have Samuel identify the patterns in classroom routines, student response patterns, and how Samuel responds to students. From these patterns, Martin and Samuel are in a position to start reconstructing the events and develop alternate strategies to focus students.

Tool 32   Tracking Student Behavior

Angle: Narrow

Focus: Student behavior

Teacher: Samuel Ortiz   **Observer:** Martin Scott

Date of Observation: May 6, 2011   **Start Time:** 2:20   **End Time:** 2:35

Total Observation Time: 15 minutes   **Period of the Day:** Afternoon

Number of Students Present: 18   **Grade Level:** 6th grade

Class: 6th grade   **Topic of the Lesson:** Language arts (Verbs)

Date of Postobservation Conference: May 7, 2011

Time	Teacher	Student
2:20	"Look at the Word of the Day on the board and write a sentence using the word. The word today is 'catastrophe.'"	"Just one sentence or two?"
2:20	"One sentence, like we do every day."	"We didn't do a word yesterday."
2:20	"OK, then, like the one we did a few days ago."	
2:21	"Tom, read your sentence."	"I'm not done...I came in late."
2:22	"Randy, let's hear your sentence."	"My pen is out of ink...I can say the sentence I would have written."
2:22	"Randy, this is the third time this week you have not come to class prepared to work."	"Yeah, yeah, yeah. I only have pencils."
2:22	"That's right...you can only use a pen to write class notes."	"I don't like pens...you can't erase the marks."
2:23	"Pens are what you must use...What don't you understand about this?"	"Why can't I use a pencil...But Mrs. Elbertson lets us use pencils...so do all my teachers, but you."
2:23	"That's right, young man, you stand out in the hall for the next 15 minutes. Go to the office...now."	
2:24	"Does anyone want to read their sentence?"	Three hands go up.
2:25	"Leslie, go ahead and read your sentence."	"After several attempts, the sailors were able to avoid a catastrophe at sea."
2:25	"Excellent sentence, Leslie."	

Continued

Time	Teacher	Student
2:26	"Pull out your grammar books and go to page 89. Make sure your notebooks are ready for class notes."	Students begin to pull out books from book bags. Two students (girls in third row, far right) begin to pull out a book; students to their right exchange books and a notebook.
2:29	"Go to Sentence 5, 'The children seated at the table began asking for dessert.' Look at the word 'seated.' Can this word be the verb in this sentence?"	Hands go up, teacher asks Joey (his hand not raised) to answer the question. Laughter with other hands starting to go up.
2:29	"Joey, what is your answer?"	"Yes."
2:29	"Why all the laughter? And Joey, look at the sentence again."	
2:30	"What is a participle?"	About nine hands go up; four students looking in book for the answer; five students looking around the room.
2:31	"Anna"	"A word that ends in 'ed,' 'en,' 'n,' or 'ing.'"
2:31		Boy shouts out "Not!"
2:32	"Tony, why 'not'?"	"What about 'the man died'—isn't died a verb in that sentence and it ends in 'ed'?" Students in the third row are talking.
2:33	"That's right in the sentence Tony gave you. But look back at Sentence 5...The word is "seated." The word "seated" is really functioning as what?" Teacher does not call on students to answer. He begins to "teach." "Let's consider a few points: "Pure grammatical rules do not always apply—you have to look at the sentence and how each word is being used. "A participle is more than a word that has a certain ending. A participle is usually a multiworded adjective... "Let's look at the proof to determine if a word is an adjective."	Hands fly up...students want to answer...they are making sounds ("ooh, ooh, ooh").
2:35	"What is the proof to see if a word is an adjective?"	Jackson answers: "Whose, which, what kind of, how many."

Classroom Traffic

Background

The classroom is often marked by the movement of teachers and their physical proximity with students. Movement could include movement during a lecture while checking on student progress during independent work or work in cooperative groups and during demonstrations. Because of content, some classes require more movement for teachers and students. Think of the fast-paced nature of instruction in the gym, a consumer science course (i.e., sewing or foods lab), a band or choral room, and even the "traditional classroom" where demonstrations occur. Teachers seek feedback regarding their own movement and often the movement of their students. Teachers may wonder if there are any "blind" spots or areas of the classroom in which students are not being attended to during the instructional period. Tracking classroom traffic gives teachers insight on their movements during class.

Observation Focus: teacher movement around the room and contact with students

Observation Technique: narrow lens

Explanation of the Tool and Technique: This tool allows the principal, supervisor, or coach to track the movement of the teacher and/or students during an observation. Using a seating chart, the observer uses lines to track these movements.

How and Why the Technique Is Helpful: The teacher and the observer are able to recreate the movement throughout the time in which the observation occurs.

Directions and Approaches for Using the Tool: On a seating chart (Tool 33, page 80), use lines to track the movement of the teacher. Use arrows to show the direction of the teacher's movement. Note the time along each line, so that not only the movement but also the length of time the teacher works with each student can be tracked.

Tips: Tool 33

♦ To reduce the amount of "noise" on any one diagram, use more than one seating chart for an extended classroom observation, notating the start and end time at the top of each.

♦ Record anecdotal notes in the margins or on another sheet of paper.

♦ Use the same seating chart to note the classroom traffic of certain students. Use different colors or different types of lines to show the movement of individual students.

Suggested Postobservation Conference Strategies: Tool 33

With the seating chart as a backdrop for the postobservation conference, lead the teacher into "seeing" the patterns of movement. Probing questions could include:

♦ Which students did you spend a majority of the time working with?

♦ Were there students who did not need assistance?

Tool 33   Classroom Traffic—Seating Chart

Angle: Narrow

Focus: Teacher moving around the room and contacting students; teacher proximity

Teacher: Shirley West

Observer: Paula Aguilar

Date of Observation: April 28, 2011

Start Time: 7:45   **End Time:** 8:00

Total Observation Time: 15 Minutes

Period of the Day: 1st Hour

Number of Students Present: 18

Grade Level: Mixed 10th and 11th

Class: Algebra II

Date of Postobservation Conference: April 29, 2011

Topic of the Lesson: Hyperbolas—How to graph and write equations of hyperbolas that consist of two vaguely parabola-shaped pieces that open either up or down

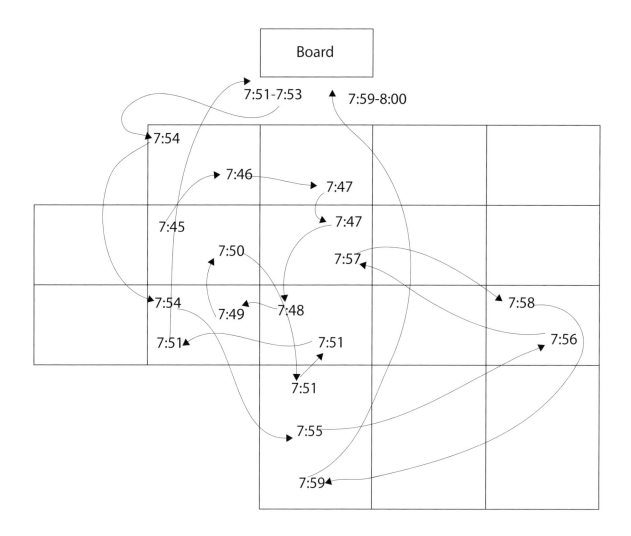

Tracking the Beginning and Ending (Closure) of Class

Background

Effective teachers engage in bell-to-bell instruction. The first few minutes and the last few minutes are acknowledged as two critically important points of time. Research shows that time wasted at the beginning and ending of class can never really be recouped; once time is lost, it is gone. Effective teachers establish daily routines for the beginning and ending of class, and grade level dictates the types of routines established. Although there are vast differences among elementary, middle, and high school classrooms, all share a commonality: the need for routines to begin and end instruction.

Beginning Class Routines

Teachers who have routines for the beginning of a class period use the time immediately before the tardy bell getting students ready and organized for learning. Strategies to maximize time on task and to reduce "empty air time" before formal instruction begin include taking attendance as students are entering the room; having a "sponge" activity, such as a short quiz or math problem, for students to start working on as they arrive; posting the day's agenda and what materials to get ready before the bell rings; and distributing class materials and collecting homework. All of these activities help to prepare students, so that the moment the bell rings, instruction or other activities related to the lesson can begin.

Ending Class Routines

Effective teachers use the time immediately before the ending of a class period to review lessons learned and help bring closure to the class activities. They relate what needs to be done to prepare for the next day so that, once the bell rings, students can be dismissed. Different cues give students time to put away supplies and equipment and get ready to leave the class in an orderly manner.

Observation Focus: activities within the first 15 minutes of class or the last 15 minutes of the class

Observation Technique: narrow focus, using anecdotal notes

Explanation of the Tool and Technique: The principal, supervisor, or coach will want to examine the routines used to begin or to come to closure of the class.

How and Why the Technique Is Helpful: This anecdotal technique allows the observer to chronicle activities that support bell-to-bell instruction at two key times during the class period—the beginning and ending of the instructional period. This technique focuses data collection on the events and instructional activities at either the beginning or the ending of the period to assess how time is being used to focus student learning.

Directions and Approaches for Using the Tool: Chronicle the activities and procedures the teacher uses to begin or end class instruction. Note the amount of time it takes the teacher to open or close class, paying particular attention to the routines, student familiarity with routines, and the cues the teacher uses to signal students.

Tool 34   Beginning of Class Routines

Angle: Narrow

Focus: Activities within the first 15 minutes of the class

Teacher: Amy Kleibar   **Observer:** Sou Chen

Date of Observation: May 6, 2011   **Start Time:** 8:05   **End Time:** 8:20

Total Observation Time: 15 minutes   **Period of the Day:** Period 1

Number of Students Present: 23   **Grade Level:** 9th grade

Class: English 1   **Topic of the Lesson:** (NA due to focus on beginning of class routines)

Date of Postobservation Conference: May 7, 2011

Time	Beginning of the Period	Student Behavior
8:05	Attendance is taken as students enter the room. Teacher [T] is in the doorway, stopping students as they enter, reminding students to take off coats and hats.	Students entering the room and stopping by T's desk to pick up graded papers; students comparing grades as they walk to their desks (clusters of students clog the doorway and area around T's desk).
8:07	Bell rings. T closes door and picks up papers left on desk—calls students up to the front of the room to pick up papers.	Students sitting at desk, while T gives students their papers; student in row 3 trips a student; two students in row 5 push around books, while walking up the aisles.
8:08	Announcements from the activities office are given; T opens the door for late students and stops at the computer station to log tardy students.	Students sitting at desk: nine students turned around talking to other students during announcements; five students are digging materials out from their book bags; three students lined up at the pencil sharpener.
8:11	T cues students to review due dates for next essay—points to the board and tells students, "Get these dates in notebooks."	Students start opening notebooks: three are trying to borrow paper (no notebooks).
8:12	T cues students, "Review my comments on your papers. Revisions are due tomorrow—rewrite only the parts of the essay circled in green."	Students start thumbing through essays...one student asks what to do if there are no "green circles." Lots of laughter.
8:13	T cue: "It's a bit noisy in here today ... Let's begin by reviewing the elements of an introductory paragraph, but first pull out Writing Tip Sheet 3 from your writing folders."	Students begin looking in book bags for writing folders...several begin to move closer to one another.

Continued

Time	Beginning of the Period	Student Behavior
8:14	T offers copies of Writing Tip Sheet to three students who do not have this sheet…gives out sheet to 13 students	A student asks, "Are we going to finish our group activity from yesterday?"
8:14	T: "First, we're going to review the elements of an introductory paragraph … review silently for a moment the key elements of an introductory paragraph."	Students start to read the sheet.
8:15	T walks around the room as students read Writing Tip Sheet	Students are quietly reading sheet.
8:18	T turns on overhead…overhead has a sample introductory paragraph written by the student who had "no green circles" on his paper; teacher cues students to the paragraph and asks them to (1) read the paragraph, (2) compare the elements of an introductory paragraph to the sample on the overhead, and (3) write a few thoughts about the sample paragraph related to the elements found on Tip Sheet 3.	Students focus on the paragraph, quietly reading it…many students are writing notes in notebook…a few students are talking with their neighbors…talk is quiet.
8:19– 8:20	T is walking around the room monitoring.	

Tips: Tool 34 and Tool 35

◆ Record data in one- to two-minute increments.

◆ Record major events in detail. A few strong examples with complete and accurate information will make more sense than trying to record extraneous information.

◆ Leave a space, such as a large column in the margin, for use during the postobservation conference to make notes (e.g., teacher analysis, questions, concerns, or ideas).

Suggested Postobservation Conference Strategies: Tool 34

Lead the teacher through looking for patterns in:

◆ traffic patterns before the start bell rings

◆ routines for getting started

Text continues on page 86.

Tool 35 Tracking End of Class Routines

Angle: Narrow

Focus: Activities within the last 15 minutes of the class

Teacher: Amy Kleibar

Observer: Sun Chen

Date of Observation: May 6, 2011   **Start Time:** 8:45   **End Time:** 9:00

Total Observation Time: 15 minutes   **Period of the Day:** Period 1

Number of Students Present: 23   **Grade Level:** 9th grade

Class: English I   **Topic of the Lesson:** (NA due to focus on beginning of class routines)

Date of Postobservation Conference: May 7, 2011

Time	Ending of the Period	Student Behavior
8:45	Teacher is moving from group to group, speaking with students, examining work.	Students are in small groups discussing essays.
8:48	Teacher cues students to move desks back in place for large-group processing.	Students start to break out of groups by moving desks back in rows...minimal noise...a student from each group is putting books (thesaurus, dictionary, etc.) back on teacher's desk.
8:49	Teacher is in front of the room readying for instruction...makes a few statements: (1) "Please bring notebooks tomorrow, and I'll add more information about the essay." (2) "Also, rewrites on the areas circled in green are due tomorrow, just rewrite the sections circled in green."	Student desks are in a row and students are listening to the teacher, quietly.
8:50	"Let's recap the importance of the advanced organizer in the introductory paragraph and how this organizer serves as a transition to subsequent paragraphs."	Students sit quietly for about 10 seconds...hands start going up.
8:50	"Jamie..."	"The organizer is the road map and helps the writer point to the major points that get discussed in the essay...in a way it's a writer's compass..."

Continued

Time	Ending of the Period	Student Behavior
8:51	"That's an interesting metaphor...a compass...is there any other value to a compass?"	Fred responds, "The organizer is for the reader, too...the compass helps the traveler know what direction he is in...going..."
8:52	"Excellent parallel...let's look at a sample from an essay." Teacher flips the overhead on and focuses students to the advanced organizer sentence that is in all bold on the screen. "Look at this advanced organizer...comment on its importance and value...Lauren, what do you think?"	Lauren responds, "This organizer has three items in it...the symbols in the book (1) help to illustrate the deeper meaning, (2) provide an understanding of what motivated the main character, and (3) foreshadow the ending of the book."
8:54	"Superb...now what does the writer need to do next...?"	Several hands go up.
8:55	"Jackson, what do you think?"	"Take time to write another sentence or two...the organizer acts as a segue to the next paragraphs." Student asks a question: "Does the advanced organizer have to always have three points?"
8:56	"Actually, the number of points is not important because..."	Student responds: "It depends on what the essay is trying to get across."
8:56	"That's correct...And we'll be reviewing several more introductory paragraphs tomorrow...let's recap from the day..." Teacher highlights the Tips for Writing Introductory paragraphs, the uses and misuses of advanced organizer and the purpose of the advanced organizer.	Students are listening and taking notes. Three students are starting to pack up their materials. Teacher cues disapproval by standing by the desk of one student. The others stop packing up their materials.
9:00	Bell rings and teacher thanks the class for working hard and wishes them well for the rest of the day.	Students pack up their bags and start leaving the room.

- ♦ student familiarity with routines
- ♦ verbal and nonverbal cues the teacher gives to students

Tool 35 helps the principal, supervisor, or coach collect data toward the end of an instructional period.

Suggested Postobservation Conference Strategies: Tool 35

Lead the teacher through looking for patterns in student familiarity with closure routines, verbal and nonverbal cues the teacher gives to students, use of strategies to summarize and come to closure, and orderly dismissal.

Cooperative Learning Groups

Background

Cooperative learning is an instructional model in which students complete work collaboratively in small groups. The work of a cooperative learning group is structured so that each group member contributes to the completion of the learning activity. Cooperative learning group work is sometimes chaotic, with students talking to one another, perhaps even across groups, comparing answers, quizzing one another, or securing materials from bookshelves. In cooperative learning, students assume a variety of active roles, including leader, time keeper, runner, recorder, and presenter. Because the cooperative learning structures encourage not only the content of what is being learned, but also social and leadership skills, the teacher encourages students to rotate roles. Figure 4.2 outlines common roles students assume in cooperative learning structures and the tasks of the student assuming these roles.

Because the work of the recorder is different from the work of the runner, the principal, supervisor, or coach needs to realize that students in cooperative learning groups are engaged in a variety of ways doing things differently throughout the duration of the group's time together.

FIGURE 4.2: Cooperative Learning Roles

Role	Tasks
Leader	Ensures all group members have the opportunity to participate fully; focuses discussions and activities around the primary group task
Time Keeper	Keeps an eye on the clock, keeping members on task; gives the group reminders at mid- and ending points of time left to accomplish tasks
Runner	Ensures the group has materials to accomplish tasks; leaves the group at peak times to get materials or ask the teacher for assistance or clarification
Recorder	Records the group's work; keeps track of key ideas
Presenter	Presents the group's work to larger group

Observing in a classroom using cooperative group structures will look very different than a classroom where the teacher is lecturing, for example. The directions the teacher provides, the monitoring the teacher does within and across groups, and the eye to time on task are essential for cooperative learning to be successful. In cooperative learning, the teacher assumes responsibility for monitoring students' learning and intervening within the groups, and teaching begins well before the class meets.

Depending on when the observer enters the room, a variation of data collection includes using anecdotal notes across the categories that Johnson and Johnson (1994) identified as essential to framing cooperative learning. Tool 36 can help the principal, supervisor, or coach script anecdotal notes while observing in a classroom where cooperative learning is being used.

Tool 36 Focus on Cooperative Learning

Angle: Narrow

Focus: Student interaction and teacher monitoring

Teacher: Theresa Lipinski   **Observer:** Carol Overman

Date of Observation: April 30, 2011   **Start Time:** 1:50   **End Time:** 2:10

Total Observation Time: 20 minutes   **Period of the Day:** 7th period

Number of Students Present: 23   **Grade Level:** Freshman (Honors)

Class: English 1   **Topic of the Lesson:** Romeo and Juliet

Date of Postobservation Conference: May 1, 2011

Focus	Notes
Objectives for the cooperative learning group	Objectives for the lesson were on the board with direction for students to form groups.
Clarity of directions	Teacher restated the directions before students moved into groups.
Transitions from small to large group work	Teacher cued the students with "two minutes left!"
Monitoring and intervening strategies	Teacher walked around the room and moved from group to group.
Evaluation strategies	N/A
Interactions with students	Called students by name; very respectful.
Follow-up instruction	N/A

Observation Focus: student interaction and teacher monitoring

Observation Technique: narrow lens focusing on the work of students in groups and the teacher's monitoring strategies

Explanation of the Tool and Technique: The cooperative learning model is dependent on small-group work. Tool 37 will assist in tracking not only the work of students, but also how a teacher tends to the work of students in small groups.

How and Why the Technique Is Helpful: Through monitoring the group activities, the teacher will be able to determine individual student involvement (Johnson & Johnson, 1994). The observer can assist teachers in assessing the work of students, individually or in groups, by collecting data on what students are doing and how students are interacting with one another in cooperative learning groups.

Directions and Approaches for Using the Tool: Once students are in groups, record the interactions of students and the strategies the teacher uses to monitor the work of students within groups.

Tips: Tool 37

- ◆ Track teacher movement from group to group.

- ◆ Record teacher verbal cues, such as directions for the groups prior to and during cooperative group activities.

- ◆ Depending on the situation, the principal, supervisor, or coach should feel free to walk around the room to hear students interact with one another and the teacher's cues redirecting student focus and get a better sense of what strategies the teacher uses to intervene in the work of small groups.

- ◆ The principal, supervisor, or coach can also focus on one collaborative learning group, if there is something about a group that catches his or her attention.

Suggested Postobservation Conference Strategies: Tool 37

Ask the teacher to look for his or her patterns of monitoring and moving from group to group. Have the teacher analyze the time he or she spent working with individual groups. Tool 38 shows an alternative approach to collecting data related to cooperative learning.

Suggested Postobservation Conference Strategies: Tool 38

Ask the teacher to review patterns associated with giving directions and clarifying information, the amount of time to get into cooperative groups, and movement from group to group.

Tool 37   Cooperative Learning—Student Interactions and Teacher Monitoring

Angle: Narrow

Focus: Student interaction and teacher monitoring

Teacher: Theresa Lipinski   **Observer:** Carol Overman

Date of Observation: April 30, 2011   **Start Time:** 1:50   **End Time:** 2:10

Total Observation Time: 20 minutes   **Period of the Day:** 7th period

Number of Students Present: 23   **Grade Level:** Freshman (Honors)

Class: English 1   **Topic of the Lesson:** Romeo and Juliet

Date of Postobservation Conference: May 1, 2011

Group	Number in Group	Student Interaction	Teacher Monitoring Strategies
1	4	Discussing the use of foreshadowing—one student recording comments; one student finding supporting citations from the text; two students talking with one another	Teacher with Group 4
2	3	Two students reading book, scanning for citations—no talking; one student sketching a crest for the Montague family	Teacher physically with Group 4 but "eye scanning" Group 5
3	4	One student asking questions; one student writing responses; one student doodling in notebook (Capulet crest); one student reading biology book	Teacher moves to Group 5; teacher speaking with group members—full attention to Group 5
4	4	Students reading text and alternately speaking with one another...one student starts to draw the family crest for the Capulets	Teacher stays with Group 5 for four minutes
5	4	Two students talking loudly; one student looking in book bag; one student talking to a student in Group 6	Teacher "making eye contact" from position in with Group 4...teacher breaks in with an announcement (eight minutes left for group work)
6	4	Two students sharing a book; one student trying to borrow colored pencils for the crest (Capulet); one student reading teacher handout	Teacher now walking around the room, moving from Group 1 to Group 2. Teacher announces four minutes left, asks for a volunteer group to share artistic rendition of the family/royal crest. Teacher moves to the front of the room to set up the overhead projector and CD player. Teacher moves back to Group 5, asks for examples of foreshadowing, calls time by asking the question: "How does Shakespeare use foreshadowing from scene 2 forward?" Students start to move desks around to break out of groups.

Looking In

Tool 38   Tracking Teacher Behaviors Promoting Cooperative Learning

Angle: Narrow

Focus: Teacher behavior; cooperative learning

Teacher: Janie Adams   **Observer:** Brenda Arlin

Date of Observation: April 25, 2011   **Start Time:** 9:05   **End Time:** 9:25

Total Observation Time: 20 minutes   **Period of the Day:** 2nd period

Number of Students Present: 26   **Grade Level:** Juniors

Class: U.S. History   **Topic of the Lesson:** Examining how a bill is passed

Date of Postobservation Conference: April 28, 2011

Focus on Cooperative Learning	Presence or Absence	Notes
Objectives for the cooperative learning group	X	✓ Objective for the activity was written on the whiteboard ✓ Teacher referred to the objective as students asked questions. ✓ Teacher returned to the objective during closure of group activity.
Clarity of directions	X	✓ Before breaking students into groups, teacher gave directions. ✓ Teacher distributed directions for each group once students moved into their groups.
Movement into groups	X	✓ Six minutes were given for students to move into groups. ✓ Materials were bundled for each group in advance of movement.
Monitoring and intervening strategies	X	✓ Teacher turned lights on and off to get attention. ✓ Teacher broke into group time three times with clarifying directions. ✓ Teacher visited each group four times.
Evaluation Strategies		
Interaction with students	X	✓ Teacher asked questions and gave feedback to groups, while monitoring. ✓ Teacher clarified directions. ✓ Teacher became a member of each group.
Follow-up instruction—large-group processing	X	✓ After 19 minutes, teacher called end to group work. ✓ Students moved desks and chairs back in order. ✓ Group reporter gave report. ✓ Teacher asked and answered questions.

Technology Implementation and Integration

Background

Technology in the form of computers and peripheral components has been in place in schools since the 1970s. Technology can bring the outside world into a classroom. Advances in technology and its availability have changed the way many teachers forward instruction and support student learning. Technology can be used to differentiate instruction, particularly in small-group or individualized instruction. Used in classroom activities, technology can be used to explore our universe and provide instructional support through games, reviews, simulations, and tutorials—all to extend learning opportunities by enhancing critical thinking and problem-solving skills.

However, just having access to computers and software in a classroom does not ensure technology integration. Teachers need to purposefully plan for technology integration, and observers can provide feedback on these efforts and extend discussions with teachers attempting to integrate technology with their teaching. According to a report of the Northwest Regional Educational Laboratory (NREL, n.d.), technology can be integrated by using an integrated learning system in a subject; allowing, encouraging, or requiring students to use word processing and presentation software in reports and displays; requiring papers be done on a word processor; using presentation software and projection technology for teacher presentations; and using computers for online testing and analysis of test results (p. 1). NREL asserts that technology integration is occurring, if teachers are trained in a full range of technology uses and in the determination of their appropriate roles and applications and students, along with teachers, routinely turn to technology when needed and are empowered and supported in carrying out those choices (p. 2). Finally, NREL offers that there are certain actions and characteristics that teachers exhibit to promote technology integration. These actions and characteristics not only occur in the classroom, but are also apparent in the planning and design of lessons and interactions among teachers:

- ♦ Teachers use technology in several ways, and such use is observable daily.

- ♦ Teachers routinely choose the technologies appropriate to their activity and need.

- ♦ Teachers are using online access to information resources from within the school, as well as from home or other outside settings.

- ♦ Teachers often share promising or successful practices among other teachers.

- ♦ Teachers participate in the process of developing guidelines for technology standards in curriculum areas.

- ♦ Teachers follow guidelines for technology use in the curriculum.

- ♦ Teachers involve students in identifying how technology may be used to accomplish curricular objectives.

♦ Teachers expect and encourage the independence of students in choosing and using technologies appropriate to their tasks.

♦ Teachers design assignments for students based on assumptions of technology use. (p. 5)

Observation Focus: how technology is integrated within teaching

Observation Technique: Mixed methods of data collection are used, including a checklist and running anecdotal notes throughout the classroom observation.

Explanation of the Tool and the Technique: Data are collected using a mixed-method approach detailed in the Classroom Observation Guide to Track Technology Integration (Tool 39).

How and Why the Technique Is Helpful: This tool allows the principal, supervisor, or coach to observe how technology is being integrated throughout instruction and how students are engaging in technological applications. The tool is flexible enough to support recording open-ended notes to chronicle the uses of technology.

Directions and Approaches for Using the Tool: Script notes as events in the classroom unfold. Check off items in the Classroom Observation Guide to Track Technology Integration tool (Tool 39) related to technology integration within the structure of the lesson being observed.

Tips: Tool 39

♦ Take detailed, scripted notes, and use the scripted notes to extend discussion.

♦ Note not only how technology is integrated by the instructor, but also how students are using technology, either in groups or independently.

Suggested Postobservation Conference Strategies: Tool 39

Focus more on the scripted notes, seeking clarification on how technology and its integration is supporting the curriculum and extending student learning. Focus attention on next steps: how the students' experience will be extended to other learning opportunities in upcoming class sessions. Seek clarification of how technology and its integration is supporting the curriculum and extending student learning. Focus attention on how the teacher will extend the students' experience to other learning opportunities in upcoming class sessions.

The following are a few questions to help guide the discussion:

1. In the end, what will students do with the answers to their questions? Will they share the information with one another? If so, will students use technology, such as developing a PowerPoint presentation? Share Web sources?

2. What is the next step in this lesson?

Tool 39   Classroom Observation Guide to Track Technology Integration

Angle: Narrow

Focus: How technology is integrated within teaching

Teacher: *Art Roberson*

Observer: *Cindy Fields*

Date of Observation: *September 8, 2011*

Start Time: *10:10*   **End Time:** *10:30*

Total Observation Time: *20 minutes*

Period of the Day: *Morning Block*

Number of Students Present: *17*

Grade Level: *7th*

Class: *Social Studies*

Topic of the Lesson: *Immigrants and Ellis Island*

Date of Postobservation Conference: *September 9, 2011*

Indicators for Technology Integration

Rate each of the following using this rating scale:

   1 = Little evidence of technology use

   2 = Some evidence that technology is used in limited amounts and with simple tasks—more productivity oriented

   3 = Evidence that teacher uses technology and provides assistance to students with spreadsheets, word processing, demonstrations

   4 = Teacher is comfortable with technology use; a variety of technology is used daily, and technology is an integral part of classroom instruction

   5 = Not applicable to the lesson

5 1. Students use computers for drill and practice activities; use of stand-alone computer software.
   - Use of networkable programs, such as Accelerated Reader and Accelerated Math
   - Use of instructional Web-based software, such as Riverdeep

4 2. Students use computers for instructional purposes.
   - Use of computers for performance assessments, such as PowerPoint and Excel
   - Use of computers for Web-based research using computers to gather data
   - Use of a combination of software and Web-based research to analyze data and draw conclusions
   - Taking data and conclusions and presenting it using some type of multimedia presentation

4 3. Teacher uses presentation software, such as PowerPoint during instruction.

4 4. Teacher uses projection tools during instruction.
   - Uses overhead projector
   - Uses multimedia projector
   - Uses multimedia projector with VCR
   - Uses multimedia projector with SmartBoard or ActivBoard

Continued

_5_ 5. Teacher incorporates the use of other devices during instruction.
- Digital camera
- Scanner
- iPod
- Graphing calculators

_4_ 6. Teacher incorporates technology within the lesson, and student work is indicative of seamless transitions between traditional instruction and technology integration.

Classroom Observation Running Notes

10:10–10:15:   Mr. Roberson spent approximately five minutes recapping information from the prior day: What occurred once immigrants arrived at Ellis Island (docking, medical exams), the large numbers of immigrants that arrived at Ellis Island between 1892 and 1924 (about 22 million), etc.

10:10–10:15:   Pulls up a PowerPoint presentation that has several Web addresses for students to mark in their browsers, and he directs student pairs to go to the computers in the back of the room. Students already know their "pairs" and proceed to the back of the room. Computers are already "booted up." Directs students to type the URL http://teacher.scholastic.com/activities/immigration/tour/index.htm and then wait for further directions. Roberson ensures students have the URL plugged in and are on the virtual tour of the Ellis Island home page.

10:10–10:18:   Directs pairs to begin the tour with the audio off and to click on each tour page (approximately seven "click points"). At the end of the tour, students are asked to click onto the immigration home page URL. Students are directed to read and review Yesterday and Today. Students are reading and reviewing these pages.

10:10–10:23:   Mr. Roberson asks students to return to their seats. Explains the next project: "In pairs, come up with three questions you have about the Ellis Island experience, and write these questions on a sheet of paper."

10:10–10:28:   Calls time. Asks a person from each pair to share their questions. Mr. Roberson is at the front of the room, typing in the questions of each group. Develops a "master list" of questions.

10:10–10:30:   Asks pairs to go to the computers and begin a Google search to try to find answers to the questions. Students return to their computers with notebooks and begin searching the Web for resources to answer their questions.

10:10–10:30:   Observation ends.

The Classroom Observation Guide to Track Technology Integration Tool was developed by Ann G. Haughey, as part of her coursework in supervision theory, and her problem of practice, while working toward her specialist in education degree at the University of Georgia. Ann G. Haughey is the technology coordinator for Wilkes County Schools (Washington, GA). Used with permission.

Wide Angle: No Focus

Background

Some teachers might want to get a general idea of how things are going in the classroom. The wide-angle lens enables the principal to observe what occurs in the classroom.

Observation Focus: open-ended, no focus

Observation Technique: Anecdotal notes are taken as instruction and classroom activities unfold.

Explanation of the Tool and Technique: The observer writes as much information as possible, chronicling the activities, instructional methods in use, transition strategies, words said by the teacher or students, and any other details to provide a broad view of what was observed.

How and Why the Technique Is Helpful: Sometimes teachers just want to know what was generally occurring during specific periods of instruction.

Directions and Approaches for Using the Tool: Indicate time, and then chronicle what occurred during the specified time. It is helpful to take notes in five-minute intervals, so the teacher can see patterns during the time the notes were taken.

Tips: Tool 40

- ♦ Record events in five-minute intervals.

- ♦ Record enough information, so the teacher can make sense of the overall events of the classroom.

- ♦ Include verbal statements to focus conversation during follow-up with the teacher.

- ♦ Avoid making value judgments, while chronicling what is observed.

The principal, supervisor, or coach who likes to further organize his or her observation notes can use a table with columns to record what the teacher does, what students do, and any other observation notes. See Tool 41 (page 97) for an alternate example for taking running notes with a timeline.

Suggested Postobservation Conference Strategies: Tool 40 and Tool 41

To encourage reflection, consider open-ended questions, such as: What do you think students learned during this time in the lesson? What will you do to follow up tomorrow? How can you assess what students were learning?

Tool 40 Running Notes with a Timeline

Angle: Wide

Focus: Open-ended; no focus

Teacher: Ron Kupinski

Observer: Jesse Canlu

Date of Observation: April 28, 2011

Start Time: 10:00   **End Time:** 10:21

Total Observation Time: 21 minutes

Period of the Day: Morning

Number of Students Present: 16

Grade Level: 5th Grade

Class: 5th Grade

Topic of the Lesson: Fractions

Date of Postobservation Conference: April 29, 2011

Time	Running Notes
10:05	✓ Students worked on a problem with the teacher leading students in a quick review of fractions and decimals in everyday situations (e.g., calculating sales tax). ✓ Had students work on a sample problem.
10:10	✓ Students worked at their desks—the students who needed additional help put their notebooks on the floor—this is the cue for Mr. Kupinski to go to their desks (about five students clustered in the back put their notebooks on the floor within one minute of starting the sample problem).
10:14	✓ Mr. Kupinski reviewed skills (adding fractions—like denominators and unlike denominators) ✓ Showed students how to add two mixed numbers whose fractions have the same denominator (used an overhead and then showed some computer-generated slides on a PowerPoint) ✓ Teacher: "Franklin, where is your head at today? Can't you figure this out?" [Franklin stops talking but slams pencil down...teacher stops teaching and writes in a notebook].
10:19	✓ Provided practice with students working adding two mixed numbers whose fractions have the same denominator

Tool 41 Alternative Approach to Running Notes with a Timeline

Angle: Wide

Focus: Open-ended; no focus

Teacher: Ron Kupinski   **Observer:**

Date of Observation: April 28, 2011   **Start Time:** 10:00   **End Time:** 10:21

Total Observation Time: 21 minutes   **Period of the Day:** Morning

Number of Students Present: 16   **Grade Level:** 5th grade

Class: 5th grade   **Topic of the Lesson:** Fractions

Date of Postobservation Conference: April 29, 2011

Time	Teacher	Students	Other
10:05	Had students work on a sample problem	Students worked on a problem with the teacher leading students in a quick review of fractions and decimals in everyday situations (e.g., calculating sales tax).	
10:10		Students worked at their desks	The students who needed additional help put their notebooks on the floor—this is the cue for Mr. Kupinski to go to their desks (about five students clustered in the back put their notebooks on the floor within one minute of starting the sample problem)
10:15	Mr. Kupinski reviewed skills (adding fractions—like denominators and unlike denominators). Showed students how to add two mixed numbers whose fractions have the same denominator (used an overhead and then showed some computer-generated slides on a PowerPoint) "Franklin, where is your head at today? Can't you figure this out?"	[Franklin stops talking but slams pencil down…teacher stops teaching and writes in a notebook].	

Continued

Time	Teacher	Students	Other
10:19	Provided practice with students working adding two mixed numbers whose fractions have the same denominator	Students are working in small groups.	It seems that the students in the back need help, but the teacher works more with students sitting in the front rows.

This tool was developed by Oksana Parylo, a doctoral student at the University of Georgia, Athens. Used with permission.

Observing Interdisciplinary Teaching

Background

Interdisciplinary work in education has garnered more attention in recent years as teams of teachers work together to connect curricula to students. To support teachers in this work, school leaders can observe and nurture teachers who use an interdisciplinary approach. But what is an interdisciplinary approach to supervision, and why is such an approach important for educational leadership? An interdisciplinary approach to supervision allows for a holistic, circular approach to the importance of multiple content approaches with identified relationships between subjects (Coffey, 2010).

Jacobs (1989) defines interdisciplinary learning as "a knowledge view and curriculum approach that consciously applies methodology and language from more than one discipline to examine a central theme, issue, problem, topic, or experience" (p. 8). For teachers and students this perspective helps to conquer the inadequacies of the traditional format of separated, structured disciplines, where connections are examined and explored by teachers and students so as to overcome the complex nature of problems presented, while grasping the many perspectives needed to solve critical issues in the 21st Century (Frodeman, Klein, & Mitcham, 2010).

According to Collins, Brown, and Newman (1989), an interdisciplinary and cross-curricular approach to teaching provides a meaningful way in which students can use knowledge learned in one context as a baseline foundation for other contexts in and out of school.

An interdisciplinary approach is a more effective means of presenting curricula because "the curricula becomes more relevant when there are connections between subjects rather than strict isolation," providing "active linkages between fields of knowledge" for students (Jacobs, 1989, p. 5). Just as it is important to show students the linkages between the subjects studied in school and that which is relevant to their lives, it is important to provide symmetry for the supervision of teachers (Jacobs, 1989). Supervisors can provide the support teachers need for integrating interdisciplinary strategies into the curricula of the school through observation and discussion as a means to "help students better integrate strategies from their studies into the larger world" (Jacobs, 1989, p. 6).

Observation Focus: mixed methods tool is used to determine where and how multiple content areas are incorporated into a lesson

Observation Technique: selective verbatim with time

Explanation of the Tool and Technique: According to Jacobs (1989), despite teachers' good intentions and planning efforts, interdisciplinary courses lack staying power. To combat this lack of follow-through, supervision can support and nurture the staying power of interdisciplinary teaching efforts among teams of teachers. The purpose of the interdisciplinary tool is to provide teamed or individual teachers feedback on whether or not they are making references to other subject areas within their current curriculum. The intent of the tool is to allow teachers to view how they go about making interdisciplinary connections to other subject areas, while also highlighting student responses to these other content connections. While using the tool, there is a set of questions to consider while supervising a teacher:

♦ What subject areas are referenced by members of the teaching team? How are these subject areas referenced?

♦ How do teaching team members go about making multiple subject connections (word problems, activities, warm-up, etc.)?

♦ How and with what comments are the students responding? Do the students respond immediately or at a different point within the lesson?

Whether observing for supervision or through the self-discovery of a team of teachers, the data gathered from using this interdisciplinary tool will provide quantitative and qualitative data on whether the students and teachers are making connections to other subjects, and how these connections are made. Through the analysis of the data collected here, the team of teachers can work together to find ways to incorporate more curricula from other subject areas while still addressing the curriculum of their designated subject area.

How and Why the Technique Is Helpful: This technique allows the observer to see how interdisciplinary teaching is incorporated across different content areas.

Directions and Approaches for Using the Tool: The interdisciplinary tool is designed to gather data on references made to subject or content specialty areas in the school curriculum. To begin using the tool, it is important to mark or circle the subject area that is being observed. As the observation takes place, the supervisor is to write the comments or questions (C/Q) referenced in the column of the subject area in which there was a connection. For example, if in a social studies classroom a curricular connection is made to mathematics, the supervisor is to write the comment or question under the mathematics column.

What is needed to use this tool effectively? The observation focus must have two agreements negotiated before beginning the observation cycle: (1) a fundamental understanding of the meaning of terms to be used, and (2) a specific body of content offered from each discipline to be used in teaching practice. It is essential that "decisions regarding the curriculum be made with a deliberate consensus" (Jacobs, 1989, p. 9). Agreement will provide opportunity to practice classroom instructional time more efficiently while addressing content in greater depth. At the same time, students are given the opportunity to connect multiple content area information and engage in authentic, relevant tasks (Barton & Smith, 2000).

Tool 42   Evidence of Interdisciplinary Teaching with a Focus on Teacher's Comments and Questions and Student Responses

Angle: Narrow

Focus: Teacher's comments and questions and student responses

Teacher: Mr. Satchelmo   **Observer:** Mr. McHale

Date of Observation: 12/06/11   **Start Time:** 10:00AM   **End Time:** 10:25AM

Total Observation Time: 25 minutes   **Period of the Day:** 2nd Period

Number of Students Present: 25   **Grade Level:** 7th Grade

Class: Social Studies   **Topic of the Lesson:** Factors impacting population in Africa

Date of Postobservation Conference: 12/07/11

Note: C/Q=comments/questions; SR=student response; T=time

Math	Science	Social Studies	Language Arts	Connections
T: C/Q:	T: 10:05 C/Q: What are the characteristics of deserts, savannahs, and rain forests?	T: C/Q:	T: C/Q:	T: C/Q:
T: SR:	T: 10:05 SR: People probably would rather live in the rain forests.	T: SR:	T: SR:	T: SR:
T: C/Q:	T: C/Q:	T: C/Q:	T: 10:08 C/Q: Let's begin the project by writing a compare and contrast paper on the different climates in Africa.	T: C/Q:
T: SR:	T: SR:	T: SR:	T: 10:08 SR: How many paragraphs?	T: SR:

Continued

Math	Science	Social Studies	Language Arts	Connections
T: 10:10 C/Q: Second part of the project, make a graph displaying the pop. of people living in the different climates.	T: C/Q:	T: C/Q:	T: C/Q:	T: 10:13 C/Q: Third part of the project, draw a map of Africa and color code where the different climates are located.
T: 10:11 SR: Does the type of graph matter?	T: SR:	T: SR:	T: SR:	T: SR:

Additionally, there is a student response area in which the supervisor may note the comment or question made by the student in response to the interdisciplinary connection previously made by the teacher. Also, by noting the time the comments were made by either the teacher or the student, the supervisor and the team can analyze the response time of the students to help determine how quickly the students are making the interdisciplinary connections.

Tips: Tool 42 and Tool 43

◆ Prepare multiple copies of the tool for your observation.

◆ Create a key prior to the observation to remind you of what the abbreviations stand for on the tool.

◆ Leave the observed subject area blank to keep the focus on the curricular references made to other subject areas during the observation.

◆ Have access to a clock or other timing device.

As an alternate approach to using the tool, the supervisor may choose to focus the observation on whether or not the students are making interdisciplinary connections. With a more student-focused observation, the supervisor is to write the comments and/or questions (C/Q) made by the students, as well as the time. If the teacher responds to the comments, then an area is designated to write the teacher's response. Later, the supervisor or teacher team may reflect on how often and in what subject areas students are making interdisciplinary connections.

Suggested Postobservation Conference Strategies

From Theory to Practice: With the teaching colleague who has agreed to work with you, conduct a classroom observation using a data collection tool presented in this chapter.

Looking In

Tool 43   Evidence of Interdisciplinary Teaching with a Focus on Students' Comments and Questions and Teacher Responses

Angle: Narrow

Focus: Students' comments and questions and teacher responses

Teacher: Ms. Peaha   **Observer:** Dr. Firestone

Date of Observation: 10/20/2011   **Start Time:** 1:15PM   **End Time:** 1:40PM

Total Observation Time: 25 minutes   **Period of the Day:** 4th Period

Number of Students Present: 23   **Grade Level:** 7th Grade

Class: Mathematics   **Topic of the Lesson:** Symmetry, Line of Symmetry, Line of Reflection

Date of Postobservation Conference: 10/22/11

Note: C/Q=comments/questions; TR=teacher response; T=time

Math	Science	Social Studies	Language Arts	Connections
T: C/Q:	T: 1:20 C/Q: We learned in science about butterflies. They are symmetrical.	T: C/Q:	T: C/Q:	T: C/Q:
T: TR:	T: 1:21 TR: How are they symmetrical?	T: TR:	T: TR:	T: TR:
T: C/Q:	T: 1:21 C/Q: They are symmetrical, because both wings are identical and their body is the line of symmetry.	T: C/Q:	T: C/Q:	T: C/Q:
T: TR:	T: 1:22 TR: Where else have you seen symmetry?	T: TR:	T: TR:	T: TR:

Continued

Math	Science	Social Studies	Language Arts	Connections
T: C/Q:	T: C/Q:	T: 1:23 C/Q: The Taj Mahal is symmetrical. If you cut it in half both sides are identical.	T: C/Q:	T: C/Q:
T: TR:	T: TR:	T: 1:24 TR: Excellent reference to architecture.	T: TR:	T: TR:

Developed by Angela Kanellopoulos and Lauren Moret. Used with permission.

Group Processing: In a small group, debrief about the experience of conducting an extended classroom observation. Identify any difficulties you encountered in scheduling the classroom observation, choosing a technique, collecting data, or other steps of the process.

Reflection: Identify the most challenging aspect of conducting an extended classroom observation, and explore several ways to meet that challenge.

Looking Ahead...

Chapter 5 explores the follow-up process, feedback, and reflection with tips about the next steps that principals, supervisors, and coaches can take to enhance their efforts and provides some tools to foster productive discussion in such follow-up conversations.

Looking In

5
Talking with Teachers After Looking In

This chapter includes tools designed to help supervisors and coaches emerge as leaders while conducting informal classroom observations. The following tools are offered:

You have accomplished quite a bit so far, but only conducting informal classroom observations is not enough. The process is not complete without some type of follow-up discussion to the classroom observation, and, because this meeting is time-consuming, it is important for a principal, supervisor, or coach to develop a manageable schedule of informal classroom observations. It is better to conduct fewer observations each week that include following up with the teachers than to conduct numerous observations without follow-up discussions. This chapter explores the follow-up process, feedback, and reflection with tips about the next steps that principals, supervisors, and coaches can take to enhance their efforts.

Following Up After an Informal Observation

To develop professionally, teachers need opportunities to talk, inquire, and reflect about their practices with the assistance of a colleague. A 20-minute informal observation yields fertile data, and the follow-up process adds value to the observation conducted. The principal, supervisor, or coach demonstrates respect for the work teachers do when immediate feedback is provided—through both written and, perhaps more profound, a purposeful discussion in which the meanings of data are explored, with the teacher assuming an active role in the process.

Worst-case scenarios include the observer who leaves a note in the teacher's mailbox without any follow-up discussion, no feedback at all, or written or oral feedback that is negative in nature. The informal observation method this book promotes includes follow-up discussion but does not preclude written feedback as well. A combination of oral and written feedback is essential to promote ongoing dialogue between the teacher and the observer and an effective principal, supervisor, or coach balances both. Tool 44 (page 106) details a written feedback form that is helpful as a prompt for follow-up discussion. Some observers find it helpful to give written feedback immediately following the observation and then follow up with discussion shortly after. By giving written feedback prior to the follow-up discussion, the teacher has time to review and absorb the information. However, some may find it useful to bring the written feedback to the postobservation conference. If the teacher receives written notes from the classroom observation during the postobservation conference, time needs to be given for him or her to read them. Time and circumstances dictate which approach the observer takes.

Tool 45 (page 107) provides an alternative form to be used in the informal postobservation conference.

Postobservation Conferences

The intent of the postobservation conference is for the teacher and observer to review and analyze the data collected, reflect on meanings, discuss possible ways of improvement, and examine future possibilities for ongoing professional development and refinement of practice. First and foremost, effective postobservation conferences are time bound, place bound, and dialogue bound.

Postobservation Conferences Are Time Bound

Time is important; if too much time elapses between the observation and the conference, the data lose meaning, and teachers lose motivation to learn from the process. Timely postobservation conferences with feedback occur within 48 hours of the observation. Some observers meet with teachers immediately after the observation. To do so, the observer must plan a follow-up conversation with the teacher during a preparation

Text continues on page 108.

Tool 44   Sample Informal Postobservation Feedback Form

Purpose: A form to assist the observer during the postobservation

Teacher: Patty Braveman

Observer: Jennifer Spinks

Date of Observation: May 22, 2011

Start Time: 9:30   **End Time:** 9:50

Total Observation Time: 20 minutes

Period of the Day: 2nd period

Number of Students Present: 18

Grade Level: Mixed 9th, 10th, and 11th

Class: Spanish I

Topic of the Lesson: How to tell time in Spanish

Date of Postobservation Conference: May 23, 2011

Students were:

- ☒ working in small, cooperative groups
- ☐ making a presentation
- ☐ taking a test
- ☒ working independently at their desks
- ☐ viewing a film
- ☒ other: Pair-share groups to practice telling time in Spanish

Teacher was:

- ☒ lecturing
- ☐ facilitating a question and answer sequence
- ☐ working independently with students
- ☒ demonstrating a concept
- ☒ introducing a new concept
- ☐ reviewing for a test
- ☐ coming to closure
- ☐ other

Comments:

Patty: Wow and more Wow on your efforts to provide solid instruction and to engage a group of students in the lesson on how to tell time in Spanish. The introduction hooked students, because you: (1) used prompts (e.g., the big clock, smaller clocks for each student and their groups), (2) incorporated the use of time with prior lesson content (e.g., ordering a meal, asking for directions, making a long-distance call in a different time zone), and (3) kept the small pair-share groups focused with written directions on the oral exercise to practice before getting back into large group.

Tool 45   Alternative Informal Postobservation Feedback Form

Purpose: Alternative form to assist the observer during the postobservation

Teacher: Jane Drew   Observer: Amy Chen

Date of Observation: March 23, 2011   Start Time: 9:30   End Time: 9:50

Total Observation Time: 20 minutes   Period of the Day: 2nd period

Number of Students Present: 15   Grade Level: 5th

Class: Spanish I   Topic of the Lesson: Telling time in
                                       Spanish

Observation Focus: Teacher questions   Observation Tool Used: Bloom's
                                       Taxonomy

Place of Postobservation Conference: teacher's classroom

Date of Postobservation Conference: March 24, 2011

Instruction

- Learning objectives: What will the students learn?

  The students will learn to tell time in Spanish.

- What did instruction look and sound like? What did the teacher do and what did the students do?

  The teacher instructed; students practiced individually and in small groups.

- What instructional strategies were used?

  lecturing; concept demonstration; introducing a new concept

- What resources and materials did the teacher use throughout the lesson?

  demonstration tables; white board; overhead

Data Analysis

- What can we conclude from observational data?

  The students were explained the concept and had a chance to practice it; different techniques were used by the teacher

- What can be done to improve instruction in the future?

  Pair the students according to their abilities and assign differentiated grammar exercises

Feedback

Jane, you provided a solid instruction to students and engaged students in the lesson on how to tell the time in Spanish. The introduction hooked students, because you: (1) used prompts (e.g., the big clock, smaller clocks for each student and their groups), (2) incorporated the use of time with prior lesson content (e.g., ordering a meal, asking for directions, making a long-distance call in a different time zone), and (3) kept the small pair-share groups focused with written directions on the oral exercise to practice before getting back into large group.

period, meet with the teacher over lunch, or find a substitute for a portion of the teacher's duty period to facilitate conversation. School leaders are encouraged to become opportunistic and creative in finding time before, during, and after the day to meet with teachers for follow-up opportunities.

Postobservation Conferences Are Place Bound

The place where follow-up occurs is significant. Holding the postobservation conference in the principal's office puts the principal in a position of authority. Conducting the postobservation conference in the classroom, where the observation occurred, helps recreate the context of the learning environment. It also offers the teacher and observer appropriate and immediate props to demonstrate points made in the observation. Atmosphere is essential; the postobservation conference opens the door to future dialogue and growth. However, the library, media center, faculty lounge, and other accessible areas of the school also provide appropriate places for the observer and teacher to meet. Although privacy is essential, public places should not be avoided. The principal, supervisor, or coach who is out and about is visible, talking with teachers between classes, during duty periods, at the bus stop, at sporting events—any place where teachers are.

Postobservation Conferences Are Dialogue Bound

McGreal (1983) asserted that the more teachers talk about teaching, the better they get at it. Postobservation conferences should invite ongoing dialogue between the teacher and the principal (or other observer). Although written follow-up is acceptable in part, effort should be made to engage teachers in discussion and reflection. Not only do teachers have an opportunity to talk about their teaching and analyze data during follow-up, but they also have the opportunity to reflect on practice, express concerns, and pinpoint areas they want to pursue further with formal and informal professional development.

Lesson Reconstruction

One method, lesson reconstruction (Bellon & Bellon, 1982), elevates the teacher as an integral part of the active learning process by engaging the teacher as a learner in the process of deriving meaning from the data collected during classroom observation. The lesson reconstruction method calls for follow-up the same day, if possible. Using this method, the teacher and observer use the data to reconstruct the events of the classroom. The data drive the discussion and help the teacher reconstruct the lesson. One strategy to help lesson reconstruction is to leave the notes from the observation with the teacher when exiting the classroom (see Tool 46). Included with the raw observation notes should be the time and place of the postobservation conference to ensure that this important aspect of the informal observation does not get put on the "back burner," due to distraction caused by other responsibilities.

If the observer leaves notes with the teacher, the teacher will need time to reflect on the data and pose questions based on the observation notes. During the follow-up discussion, the teacher and observer review the notes and the corresponding questions the teacher has written on the form. The teacher and observer can engage in a discussion of the data. Although spontaneity is encouraged, the events chronicled by the observer frame the discussion. The following questions are useful in guiding the discussion:

Tool 46   Presentation of Postobservation Conference Notes

Purpose: Organization of observation notes for the postobservation conference

Teacher: Ron Kupinski

Observer: Jesse Cantu

Date of Observation: April 28, 2011

Start Time: 10:00   **End Time:** 10:21

Total Observation Time: 21 minutes

Period of the Day: Morning

Number of Students Present: 16

Grade Level: 5th grade

Class: Grade 5

Topic of the Lesson: fractions, decimals, and integers

Date of Postobservation Conference: April 29, 2011—3rd Period [Ron, I have a sub for your assigned duty period. Let's meet in the library, Jesse.]

Time	Running Notes	Teacher Questions
10:05	✓ Students worked on a problem with the teacher leading students in a quick review of fractions and decimals in everyday situations (tax).	Was my review too brisk given the observation that five students needed help within one minute of starting independent practice?
10:10	✓ Had students work on a sample problem. ✓ Students worked at their desks—the students who needed additional help put their notebooks on the floor floor—this is the cue for Mr. Kupinski to go to their desks (about five students clustered in the back put their notebooks on the floor within one minute of starting the sample problem).	
10:14	✓ Showed students to add two mixed numbers whose fractions have the same denominator (used an overhead and then showed some computer-generated slides on a PowerPoint presentation). ✓ Teacher: "Franklin, where is your head at today? Can't you figure this out? [Franklin stops talking but slams pencil down...teacher stops teaching and writes in a notebook.]	I can't get a sense of how often to review—I think they get it and then, wham, I lose two or three students. I'm thinking about appealing more to multiple intelligences...but I use overheads and other technology. Any ideas? I need help with Franklin—today he was mild.
10:19	✓ Provided practice with students working on problems related to adding mixed numbers.	

Talking with Teachers

- How do you think the lesson went?

- What went well?

- What would you do again, if you were teaching this same lesson?

- What would you do differently?

- Overall, how do you think this lesson went in comparison to the same lesson taught with a different group of students?

Again, the data and the teacher's insights will frame the discussion. This technique points to the importance of the observer's ability to chronicle data during the classroom observation.

Effective Observers Are Prepared

Being prepared for follow-up discussion with the teacher is essential; observers make judgment calls on whether follow-up should be done in writing, orally, or a combination of both. Planning time gives the principal, supervisor, or coach the opportunity to organize the raw data gathered during the observation. Teaching is fast paced, and the observer records observational data at an equally fast pace. In its final form, the data must be clear and understandable to both the teacher and the observer. To lay the groundwork for a successful postobservation conference, the principal, supervisor, or coach tackles several tasks:

- *Revisit the focus of the classroom observation.* Within the first minute or so of the informal classroom observation, the observer makes a major decision—what he or she will focus on during the length of the classroom observation. This focus determines the type of data collection method and tool that will be used. Reviewing the data, the observer looks for direct or striking examples of classroom practices that relate specifically to the chosen focus. One approach is to identify events that either contributed to or prevented the teacher from achieving an objective.

- *Develop a strategy for presenting the data collected.* Providing the teacher with objective feedback is dependent on displaying the data clearly and the ability to return to the data for clarification, explanation, or extension during the postobservation conference. The observer's role is to facilitate the teacher's reflection and self-analysis by way of the data. The conference plan should keep the teacher reflecting on and analyzing the events of the classroom and the observational data.

- *Frame an opening to get the teacher thinking and talking about teaching.* Effective invitations to dialogue, also called "icebreakers," are open-ended statements related to some aspect of teaching. The intent of an icebreaker is to get the teacher talking about events of the classroom. Conversely, conversation-stopper statements put open-ended discussions on ice. Conversation stoppers create a chill, thwarting open-ended discussions. Figure 5.1 presents examples of icebreakers and conversation-stopper statements.

FIGURE 5.1: Comparison of Postobservation
Icebreakers and Conversation-Stopper Statements

Icebreakers	Conversation Stoppers
Think back to [some aspect of the lesson or the class] and tell me about it.	Prove to me that the students were prepared for independent practice.
The approach you chose to break students into small groups helped students learn how to cooperate. Tell me how you were able to get students to this level of cooperation.	Do you think it's wise to allow your at-risk student the freedom that cooperative groups encourage?
Tell me more about _____.	Don't you think that more guided practice would have been more appropriate?
When you looked at Johnny, he knew immediately to stop talking. How did you know how and when to look at him like this? Is Johnny the only student who responds to your look to stop talking? How did you know to use that look?	Don't get too confident about Johnny—he'll talk while you are working with other students.
For the students who were absent the day before, you used activity time to help them catch up. What about the students in the activity? Can the students catch up another way?	Just analyze my notes and then get back to me if you have any questions about my assessment of your teaching.
How did you know that the student would try to…	Stop babying these kids; they are about to graduate and need to be more self-sufficient, don't you agree?

Approaches to the Postobservation Conference

To make the follow-up discussion more inviting and meaningful, a facilitative style in which the principal, supervisor, or coach is open to hearing what the teacher has to say will be most helpful to the teacher. Remember, the follow-up discussion is about the teacher, not the observer. The teacher's point of view must permeate the discussion. Talking about teaching is a cooperative endeavor. It is the observer's duty to engage the teacher in reviewing, analyzing, and reflecting on data. Through effort, patience, and willingness to assist, principals, supervisors, or coaches help teachers make progress in their professional development. To establish a collaborative relationship with the teacher, the supervisor's style and approach to communication must promote teacher talk. Figure 5.2 (page 112) identifies ways to promote teacher dialogue, inquiry, and reflection.

Feedback

Teachers need and want to know how they are doing and what they can do to improve or modify an approach to teaching; moreover, teachers need affirmation for their efforts. Data should be the only source of feedback, and the principal, supervisor, or coach should take care not to impose bias or judgment on observation data. Framing and giving

FIGURE 5.2: Approaches to Promoting Dialogue, Inquiry, and Reflection

Approach	Example
◆ Remain objective by providing the teacher with observational data that is value free and nonjudgmental. ◆ Listen more—talk less—to hear (understand) what the teacher is trying to communicate.	◆ Here are the events that led to the small group…
◆ Acknowledge, paraphrase, and ask probing and clarifying questions that encourage the teacher to talk more. ◆ Open-ended questions help the teacher make discoveries, identify recurring patterns, and reflect on possible alternatives or extensions to instructional practices. ◆ Encourage the teacher to expand on statements that share beliefs about teaching, learning, and students.	◆ Examine the following notes and tell me what responses you anticipated from students after you asked for… ◆ From your point of view, what made this lesson successful? At what point did you sense the students were "getting it"?
◆ State what went well and ask reflective questions to focus on what needs improvement from the teacher's point of view. ◆ Avoid giving directive types of advice—even if asked. Instead, engage the teacher in role-playing reprises of events you observed, then invite extended thinking. Role-playing and simulations that reflect the teacher's practices are more realistic.	◆ When the student in the red shirt said, "This is stupid," what made it possible for you to continue with activity? ◆ The small group activity really worked well. How do you think the transition back to large group could have been different? ◆ Let me pretend I am a student in your fourth hour class. How would you help me understand the concepts important to today's unit discussion?
◆ Refuse to engage in talk not related to what you directly observed or to the improvement of instruction.	◆ That thought is important. After the post-observation conference, I'll share your idea with the assistant principal.
◆ Offer to return for further observations to keep the momentum going for the teacher.	◆ When would be a good time for me to come back to see the students apply the formula?
◆ Provide ongoing support for the decisions the teacher makes in the postobservation conference by investigating with the teacher follow-up learning or enrichment activities.	◆ The district is offering an after-school workshop on higher-order thinking. Perhaps you'd like to go. Would you like me to make a reservation for you?
◆ Be aware of nonverbal behavior that can send mixed messages. Convey interest and concern.	◆ Looking at the clock, facial expressions, and body language, such as folded arms.

feedback are complicated. People want praise for their efforts, but they also want honesty when efforts need adjustment. It is often easier to give positive, rather than negative, feedback. Providing both types of feedback will require tact, wise word choice, and clear communication. Principals, supervisors, or coaches cannot afford any hidden messages in their words that can enhance or block the future efforts of the observer and teacher.

Types of Feedback

Feedback can be confirmatory or corrective, according to Kurtoglu-Hooton (2004) who details the work of Egan (2002). Based on the preliminary research of Kurtoglu-Hooton, confirmatory feedback is given in the context of praise in connection with what the teacher did well and is likely to encourage a teacher to construct his or her own constructive thought patterns and may encourage teachers to try new avenues and to pursue new challenges (pp. 1–3).

Conversely, corrective feedback is based on expected behaviors; applied to situations where there may have been a better course of action; and "a gentle telling off, " if the teacher seems to be repeating the same mistakes without any evidence of moving forward. Corrective feedback requires a period of time for the teacher to process, digest, reflect upon, and come to terms with the "criticism" involved. Kurtoglu-Hooton (2004) also asserted that confirmatory feedback is often less detailed than corrective feedback.

Feedback can be constructive or destructive. Consider the following statements:

1. "Mrs. Ritter, you really need to take the workshop. All the questions you asked were lower-level questions. Students were obviously bored with your class."

2. "Mrs. Ritter, your insight about your questions asking students for recall reminds me of how I used to ask opening questions. I benefited from the county workshop *Questioning Strategies That Promote Higher-Order Thinking*. This session is on the schedule for next month; would you be interested in attending? We have the funds and, with advance notice, I can lock in a sub for you."

Statement 1 is destructive; it is too blunt, and it puts the teacher down with a personal attack. Statement 2 communicates the same message—the teacher needs assistance with questioning strategies—but in a more productive way.

Constructive feedback provides objective insight based on data without criticizing the teacher or finding fault. This type of feedback promotes a willingness to take risks and be more open to changing practice. Destructive feedback, by contrast, belittles teachers by compiling data that point only to weaknesses or attack aspects of instruction that are beyond the teacher's control. Figure 5.3 (page 114) lists characteristics of effective feedback.

Data Overload

In an attempt to be helpful, some principals, supervisors, or coaches fall into the trap of overwhelming the teacher with too much information. Observers who attempt to establish their credibility may fall into the trap of offering a laundry list of observations based on their own view of the lesson. Supervision is not about the observer; supervision is about the teacher and the learning opportunity the data and feedback from an observation can provide. The tenor of the feedback in the postobservation conference sets the tone for future interaction between the principal, supervisor, or coach and the teacher.

Of course, even carefully framed feedback may not be well received. The way a teacher receives feedback depends on variables, such as the degree of trust between the observer and the teacher, the experience level of the teacher, the patterns of communication at the school, and the conditions surrounding the classroom observation.

Figure 5.3: Characteristics of Effective Feedback

Effective feedback in the postobservation conference:

- supports the teacher in examining both the positive and the not-so-positive aspects of practice
- creates footholds for follow-up
- nurtures a sense of worth and positive self-esteem
- facilitates self-assessment and self-discovery
- focuses on a few key areas
- accurately describes what was observed
- remains authentic and free of meaningless or patronizing platitudes
- clarifies and expands ideas for both the teacher and the observer
- deals with concrete, observed examples
- promotes goal setting and the development of strategies
- guides the teacher in thinking beyond the lesson observed
- acknowledges and incorporates the points the teacher makes as part of the feedback process

Effective feedback avoids:

- making assumptions about teachers
- overloading the teacher with detail after detail after detail
- offering global generalizations about the teacher's credibility
- judging and labeling a practice as good or bad

Feedback is effective because of its frequency, timing, specificity, and contextualized nature:

- *Frequency.* Feedback should be given often, meaning that school leaders need to get supervision "out of the main office."

- *Timing.* Feedback should be given as soon as possible after a formal or informal observation. Time fades the memory. Think of the difficulties in recreating the events of the classroom, even with stable data collected during an observation.

- *Specificity.* With stable data, feedback should be related to specific events as they unfolded in the classroom.

- *Contextualized nature.* Feedback must take into consideration classroom variables, such as the characteristics of students, the experience level of the teacher, and the focus of the classroom observation.

Feedback is critical to any instructional supervisory model. Without feedback after a classroom observation, growth and development are not likely to occur, and teachers are not likely to make changes in their classroom practices.

Next Steps

The follow-up process extends beyond the feedback and links informal classroom observations to professional development. Through a series of informal classroom observations, with written and verbal feedback, both the teacher and the school leader are aware of areas to focus on in the future. Informal classroom observations and discussions during postobservation conferences provide windows of opportunities to connect that work with professional development. Through purposeful interactions, the observer discovers skills that teachers are implementing in practice or struggling to implement; what is working in practice—how, why, or why not; the ongoing support and resources that teachers need; follow-up activities needed to support implementation; and teachers who would be willing to let others observe their teaching.

To promote professional development, the teacher and school leader should consider the following activities:

♦ attendance at workshops, seminars, and conferences

♦ observation of another teacher in the building or district

♦ enrollment in a graduate course

♦ engagement in action research with a common grade or subject area teacher

♦ formation of a study group after identifying a topic of interest

♦ development or refinement of a portfolio

The observer who seeks to learn what a teacher needs to reach the next level of performance remembers to follow through with support. With a hectic day, a large faculty, multiple tasks not related to instruction, and competing interests to focus attention on, a simple "tracking sheet" can help jog the observer's memory of teachers' interests and short- and long-term goals. A principal, supervisor, or coach in the field keeps a notebook in which he or she logs the needs of teachers based on what is observed in classrooms and the conversations he or she has with them after observations. Although it takes a couple minutes to update after every formal and informal classroom observation, this type of tracking adds credibility in that teachers know the principal, supervisor, or coach will follow through with information, opportunities, and discussions between classroom observations. Tool 47 (page 116) is a sample of what a tracking sheet might look like.

Tips: Tool 47

♦ Keep the tracking sheet simple.

♦ Put aside 10 minutes a day to update information based on the day's informal observations (even formal observations).

♦ Encourage other administrators to keep a similar type of notebook.

♦ Use a three-ring notebook and keep adding sheets for each teacher so as to have a running history that spans the teacher's career.

The possibilities are endless. Follow-up holds great promise as a supervisory tool. During this time, teachers have the opportunity to analyze and make sense of data that

Tool 47   Tracking Sheet—Faculty Needs

Purpose: Tracking the needs of the faculty

Teacher: *Jillian Clarke*   Years: *2011 to . . .*

Years at School: *12 [biology and life science]*

Short-Term Instructional Goal(s): *(1) learn more about cooperative learning related to labs*

Long-Term Instructional Goal(s): *(1) complete doctorate, (2) National Board Certification*

Log of Informal Observations

Observation Date: *09/12/11*

Follow-Up:

* *check on system offerings for cooperative learning (spring and summer)*
* *pull article, "101 Reasons for Using Cooperative Learning in Biology Teaching" (Thomas R. Lord)*
* *start subscription for The American Biology Teacher; ask the Learning Media Center director to e-mail Jillian when the issues start arriving*

Observation Date: *10/10/11*

Follow-Up:

* *check with district science coordinator about summer curriculum work and seminars available at Argonne National Laboratory*
* *check calendar for next week—Jillian requested that I do an informal observation during 6th hour on either a Monday or a Thursday to observe a lab—focus on classroom traffic and monitoring lab pairings—get seating chart*
* *note sent to custodians to get power strips in 312 and 313 (lab)*
* *check to see if Ms. Nesbitt would want to observe Jillian teach*

bring some aspect of their teaching into focus. Lesson reconstruction, as advocated by Bellon and Bellon (1982), engages the teacher in rebuilding the events of the classroom using data to analyze effectiveness. When the principal, supervisor, or coach offers objective feedback, the teacher is in a better position to make informed judgments about practice and develop further plans for growth and change.

Looking Ahead...

Chapter 6 examines how studying student work enhances the power of any discussion about what occurred in a classroom. Some techniques and tips about incorporating the examination of student work samples during a postobservation conference are explored, and some tools are provided to help gather data.

6

Studying Student Work During and After Classroom Observations

This chapter includes tools designed to help supervisors and coaches emerge as leaders while conducting informal classroom observations. The following tools are offered:

While in a classroom, the principal, supervisor, or coach should strive to keep "one eye on the teacher and the other eye on the students." Principals, assistant principals, instructional coaches, and other support personnel need to come to realize that classroom observations are about studying how students react to instruction and respond as they learn "X" from their teachers or interactions with other students and how students, teachers, and content knowledge interact—this is learning!

Through purposeful observations, principals, supervisors, and coaches see first-hand student work and artifacts of learning. Observers often see these artifacts as they are created live in the classroom. These school leaders observe students answering questions, writing problems across white boards (or blackboards), composing letters on computer screens, drawing, singing, calculating, and doing a host of other activities in which artifacts of learning are embedded.

As a strategy to support teacher learning, the examination of student work can enhance discussions during postobservation conferences. Through collaborative discussions, the meanings embedded within student work artifacts can help teachers think about their teaching and learn more about their students, as well as help teachers and leaders identify professional development opportunities. Through the process of examining student work with teachers, the observer can stimulate reflection, support change in practices, and help teachers see squarely what students are or are not learning. The analysis of artifacts of teaching—student work—can yield powerful insights about teaching while providing equally powerful learning opportunities for teachers. Sounds like a win-win situation!

Focusing on Student Work

As a strategy for teacher development, the informal classroom observation is job-embedded because the work of teaching, refining instructional practices, and meeting the needs of students coalesce into opportunities for teachers to see live the impact of efforts on student learning. Teaching and learning occur in a context—the classroom. Examining student work leads teachers to learn more about the efforts of their teaching. Some fundamental questions to think about include:

♦ What can the artifacts of teaching tell a teacher?

♦ How does a teacher make sense of student work?

♦ How many artifacts does a teacher need to know whether learning is "sticking"?

These are interesting questions that do not have "pat answers." What is known with certainty is that "when teachers analyze and discuss instructional practice and the resulting samples of student work, they experience some of the highest caliber professional development available" (The National Educational Association Foundation for the Improvement of Education, 2003, p. 2).

Although informal observations are brief, much can be observed in 15–20 minutes. The real action occurs during the discussion after the observation. There is a great deal of complexity surrounding the examination of student work. In fact, examining student work is professional development that should be sustained over time among teachers and others (Zepeda, 2008). However, there is room at the table for school leaders to engage teachers in discussions about student work and artifacts of learning as follow-up to informal and formal classroom observations. The study of student work can include many artifacts, such as essays, artwork, science experiments, blueprints, and so forth. The study of student work is a critical source of information about learning and teaching. Astute leaders purposefully seek out this type of learning opportunity for their teachers.

How Informal Classroom Observations Can Help Teachers Examine Student Work

Although most teachers can identify the gaps in their own teaching and student understanding, principals, supervisors, and coaches play a pivotal role in helping teachers examine student work samples. School leaders help teachers make sense of student artifacts, if they have collected stable data about instructional practices during informal observations. Figure 6.1 is an example of such data.

FIGURE 6.1: Data from an Informal Classroom Observation

Teacher: Shelly Beter

Observer: Julie Escobar

Date of Observation: March 4, 2011

Start Time: 9:00   End Time: 9:25

Total Observation Time: 25 minutes

Period of the Day: Block 1

Number of Students Present: 25

Grade Level: 9th grade

Class: English I (Remedial)

Topic of the Lesson: S. E. Hinton's Rumble Fish

Date of Postobservation Conference: March 4, 2011

Time	Instructional Method	Teacher Behavior	Student Activities
9:00–9:05	Organizing lecture	Lecturing, Q & A period about plot Distributing an index card to each student; Directing students to write one sentence about the importance of the Siamese fighting fish	Listening, taking notes, asking questions
9:06–9:08	Independent work	Monitoring student work	Students writing on the index cards
9:09–9:22	Large-group sharing	Teacher seeks volunteers to share insights about the Siamese fighting fish and its importance thus far in the book; asking for "proofs" from the text to support ideas written on the index cards Leading students to citations offered by groups	Sharing thoughts about the symbol of the Siamese fighting fish; finding citations from the text to support ideas
9:23–9:25	Question and answer	Asking questions	Responding to questions (looking up citations to back up ideas); asking questions

Student Work

Suggested Postobservation Conference Strategies

Later the same day, Julie Escobar visited Shelly Beter for a few minutes and asked her to review the observation notes so she could analyze the data on her own. The next day, Julie and Shelly met before school to discuss the classroom observation. Julie began the conversation with an open-ended question, "What patterns do you see in the data?"

During the postobservation conference, Julie and Shelly reviewed the various instructional strategies used, the amount of time spent on each, what students were doing during each, and what learning objectives were being met. On reflection, Shelly shared that she did not give students enough time to write out ideas and concepts on the note cards and that she would experiment with (1) extending the amount of time for note-taking and (2) giving more explicit directions to students prior to having them work independently. She also shared that some students were still having difficulties with finding "proofs" from the text of the novel. Although we know from the amount of time indicated in the observation notes that Shelly did not give students enough time to write their thoughts, we really do not know what the thoughts were and how students substantiated their thoughts with passages from the book *Rumble Fish*.

Here is the principal's cue to get the artifacts of student work into the postobservation conference. Before the postobservation conference, Julie could ask Shelly to bring the student note cards and the proofs they had written on the backs of the note cards.

Figure 6.2 illustrates how examining the note cards with the student's thoughts about the book alongside the proofs could help Shelly dig deeper into what skills her students were learning and how she could adjust her instruction to reteach how to use proofs to back up ideas found in the book.

Tool 48 can serve as a guide to examine student-generated artifacts—in this instance, the note cards and the proofs.

The objective is to look at the student work for indicators of what worked and what did not work in the lesson, but a more important priority is to encourage the teacher to look at ways to make mid-course changes in instruction. The value of timely postobservation conferences is that teachers can reflect more immediately on their practices and then make modifications, as necessary. The observer serves as the mirror for the teacher to examine instructional practices. Through this effort, teachers can identify cues on what instructional practices or curricular materials need modified.

FIGURE 6.2: Examining Student Work

Student Thought	Proofs from the Book
People are like animals.	Rusty-James said, "The animals reminded me of people" (p. 13).
	In the end, the gangs are likened to "Siamese fighting fish." They "destroy one another."
	Motorcycle Boy breaks into the pet store.
	Motorcycle Boy heads for the river shortly after the break-in at the pet store.

Tool 48   Questions to Lead the Teacher Talk about Student-Generated Artifacts

Purpose: A guide for examining student-generated artifacts

1. What information about student learning have you gleaned from the student thoughts and proofs from the cards?

2. Do students use the cards later to write essays?

3. Today, what will you do to review the proofs and the cards with students?

4. What do these artifacts tell you about what you are teaching and why?

5. If you could rework the lesson from yesterday, what would you do differently and why?

6. How can this lesson and in-class assignment be modified based on the patterns found in these cards and the proofs?

Examining student work can help teachers make better decisions related to the curriculum and its development, instructional strategies, and assessments. It would be interesting to see what Shelly would do today, based on her reflections from the previous day and the discussion during the postobservation conference.

Examining Artifacts Can Help with Further Planning

It is unlikely that Julie Escobar will be able to visit Shelly Beter's class today, but the knowledge gained from examining artifacts can serve another purpose—planning for future instruction, based on the decisions made by the teacher. Through examination of the artifacts and the other classroom observation notes, Shelly is in a position to plan out, with the live feedback from the principal, what instruction will look like for these students.

Getting Started Examining Student Work

Getting started examining student work can be awkward for teachers because they are sharing their "vulnerabilities" in full view of another person. The principal, supervisor, or coach should reassure teachers that conversations about student work are all about learning how to teach better, better develop curricular approaches, and modify instructional and curricular approaches based on what is learned while examining student work. A leader can assist teachers with the process by providing time in postobservation conferences to examine student work.

What Work to Examine?

The National Education Association Foundation for the Improvement of Education (2003) underscores that "data are more than test scores" (p. 1). Principals, supervisors, and coaches can assist teachers at the beginning stages of examining student work by

Tool 49   Thinking, Listening, and Reflecting with Colleagues about Student Work

Purpose: A protocol to be used in postobservation conference to examine student work

---

Reflecting on the Process

Looking for evidence of student thinking...

- What did you see in this student's work that was interesting or surprising?
- What did you learn about how this student thinks and learns?
- What about the process helped you see and learn these things?

Reflecting on one's own thinking...

- What questions about teaching and assessment did looking at the students' work raise for you?
- How can you pursue these questions further?
- Are there things you would like to try in your classroom as a result of looking at this student's work?

---

agreeing on a single standard (curricular/learning) and then examining student work samples that reflect that standard. Work samples could include essays, quiz or test sample responses, video clips of students completing tasks, and drawings. Any item that is a sample of student work can be studied. The objective is to study not only the artifact, but also the learning objective, the standard, and the instructional approach to see how students perform, what have they mastered, and what shifts in instructional practices need made.

How to Go About Studying Student Work

A primary objective behind studying student work is to "invite conversations about the work and the teaching associated with it" (McDonald, 2001, p. 121). However, McDonald (2001) offers that the conversations are "highly structured," employ some type of "protocol," and that "the activity of talking productively with peers about the intentions behind and the actual effects of one's work demands assertiveness and frankness but also requires delicacy and some buffer against quick judgments and harsh words" (p. 121).

McDonald (2001) believes "the discipline and structure make the process safe" (p. 122). The intent is to "suspend judgment" so "that the teacher finds her capacity to make judgments enriched by other perspectives" (p. 122). ATLAS Learning Communities, Inc. (2007) offers sound strategies to get teachers reflecting, listening, and collaborating while studying student work. Although the examination of student work often occurs among groups of teachers, the observer and the teacher can make significant gains in understanding teaching, learning, and assessment by undertaking this work. Tool 49 (adapted from one developed by ATLAS Learning Communities, Inc.) presents

Tool 50   Examining Student Work by Content Standards

Purpose: Examining student work around content standards

Teacher: _Shelly Beter_   Observer: _Julie Escobar_

Date of Observation: _March 4, 2011_   Start Time: _9:00_   End Time: _9:25_

Total Observation Time: _25 minutes_   Period of the Day: _Block 1_

Number of Students Present: _25_   Grade Level: _9th grade_

Class: _English I (Remedial)_   Topic of the Lesson: _S. E. Hinton's Rumble Fish_

Date of Postobservation Conference: _March 4, 2011_

Artifact: One student essay. Essay assignment: Develop an essay of 950 words in which two symbols from *Rumble Fish* are used to foreshadow the ending of the book. Standards: Grade 9 English.

Narrative Analysis of Grade-Level-Appropriate Text

3.3.   Analyze interactions between main and subordinate characters in a literary text (e.g., internal and external conflicts, motivations, relationships, and influences) and explain the way those interactions affect the plot.

3.7.   Recognize and understand the significance of various literary devices, including figurative language, imagery, allegory, and symbolism, and explain their appeal.

Writing Strategies

1.1.   Students write coherent and focused essays that convey a well-defined perspective and tightly reasoned argument. The writing demonstrates students' awareness of the audience and purpose. Students progress through the stages of the writing process as needed.

Organization and Focus

1.1.   Establish a controlling impression or coherent thesis that conveys a clear and distinctive perspective on the subject and maintain a consistent tone and focus throughout the piece of writing.

1.2.   Use precise language, action verbs, sensory details, appropriate modifiers, and the active, rather than the passive, voice.

Research and Technology

1.4.   Develop the main ideas within the body of the composition through supporting evidence (e.g., scenarios, commonly held beliefs, hypotheses, and definitions).

1.6.   Integrate quotations and citations into a written text while maintaining the flow of ideas.

1.7.   Use appropriate conventions for documentation in the text, notes, and bibliographies by adhering to those in style manuals (e.g., *Modern Language Association Handbook* and *The Chicago Manual of Style*).

1.8.   Design and publish documents by using advanced publishing software and graphic programs.

Continued

Questions to Guide the Examination and Discussion of the Student Essay

1. What were the objectives for the essay?
2. What content standards were being addressed?
3. What instruction was used prior to the students writing the essay?

Based on this essay:

1. What examples from the essay illustrate that the student has achieved the standard(s)?
2. What examples from the essay show there are gaps in mastery?
3. What types of instruction will be used to address these gaps? Or how will future instruction be modified?
4. What types of follow-up are provided for this student and others who do not meet the standards? Or for the students who meet or exceed the standards?

Tool 51   Planning Guide—What Next?

Purpose: Prompts to help principals talk about instruction planning

1. What content needs to be reviewed or retaught based on the discussion during the postobservation conference?

2. What instructional strategies would most likely help move learning forward to meet goals and objectives?

3. What materials are needed?

a protocol that can be used in a postobservation conference to examine student work samples and artifacts.

Another way to frame the discussion of student work is to examine content standards and the adopted curriculum for the school system. Tool 50 (page 123) provides a sample guide to help the observer frame the examination of student work around content standards adopted by the school system.

Tool 51 provides prompts to help the observer and teacher "talk through" the planning of instruction, based on the analysis of student work in the postobservation conference. Modifying questions to fit the context of the work at a given site is encouraged.

As the observer and teacher gain familiarity examining student work as part of the informal classroom observation experience, rich discussions will emerge. It is through these collaborative discussions that teaching and learning become the focus of all efforts toward increased learning for both students and teachers. This book is not advocating that all postobservation conferences include examination of student work, but rather that the examination of student work should be incorporated into discussions as appropriate.

As the school leader is out and about observing multiple teachers across grade levels and subject areas, more formalized professional development centering on student work might be worth considering. School leaders have the vantage point of knowing what is being taught and how students are responding. These insights about teaching and learning need to be shared in a way that invites teachers to consider the formal examination of student work as one way to inform instructional practices.

Looking Ahead...

The "Reproducible Classroom Tools" section (page 127) provides blank copies of the tools presented throughout this book, so the busy principal, supervisor, or coach can reproduce them to collect data during informal classroom observations.

Reproducible Classroom
Observation Tools

Tool 1   Assessing the Broad Characteristics of a Faculty

Purpose: Broadly assess the characteristics of a faculty

1. Number of teachers =   Male =   Female =

2. For each teacher, tally the number of years in teaching.

    Total number of years of experience =

    Average years of faculty experience =

3. Number of teachers whose experience falls within the following service ranges:

    a.   1 – 3 years =

    b.   4 – 7 years =

    c.   8 – 11 years =

    d.   12 – 15 years =

    e.   16 – 19 years =

    f.   20+ years =

4. Number of first-year teachers =

5. Number of teachers who retire at the end of the current school year =

6. Wildcards:

    First-year teachers with experience =

    Alternatively certified teachers =

    Teachers returning to work after an extended leave =

    Other =

7. What overall patterns do you notice?

Tool 2   Assessing Individual Teachers

Purpose: Broadly assess individual teachers

1. Teacher's name:

2. Years in education:

3. Years in the current position:

4. Years in the current school:

5. Teacher's career stage (circle one):
    a.   Preservice
    b.   Induction
    c.   Competency
    d.   Enthusiasm
    e.   Career frustration
    f.   Stability
    g.   Career wind-down
    h.   Career exit

6. Alternatively certified? If yes, in what area?

7. Other notes:

This tool was developed by Oksana Parylo, a doctoral student at the University of Georgia, Athens. Used with permission.

Tool 3   Tracking Informal Observations

Purpose: Keep a record of the conducted informal classroom observations

Teacher	Observer	Informal Observations	Date of Follow-Up	Formal Observations	Period(s)/ Time(s)	Follow-Up Topics

Tool 4   Focused Informal Classroom Observations—
Creekland Middle School

Angle: Narrow

Focus: Instructional strategies and classroom expectations

Teacher: Date:

Administrator: Class Period:

Common Classroom Expectations:

- collaboration
- differentiation
- student engagement

- summarizing
- display of student work
- essential questions (EQ)

Expectation Domains	Presence = X
1. **Assessment:** Frequently assesses students' learning of the AKS and gives specific feedback to the students and parents.	
2. **Nonverbal Representations:** Uses a variety of nonverbal/visual representations of content and skills.	
3. **Modeling and Practice:** Models strategies and skills. Provides multiple opportunities for distributed practice, followed by independent practice.	
4. **Vocabulary:** Explicitly teaches essential content-related vocabulary.	
5. **Summarizing:** Explicitly teaches students to summarize their learning.	
6. **Collaboration:** Provides collaborative learning opportunities.	
7. **Student Goal Setting:** Teaches and requires students to set personal goals for improving their academic achievement.	
8. **Literacy:** Explicitly teaches skills for improving reading and writing proficiency/ literacy across the content areas.	
9. **Problem Solving:** Uses inquiry-based, problem-solving learning strategies with students in all content areas.	
10. **Questioning:** Uses and teaches questioning and cuing/ prompting techniques.	
11. **Background Knowledge:** Accesses and/or builds students' background knowledge and experiences.	
12. **Comparison and Contrast:** Teaches students to compare and contrast knowledge, concepts, and content.	
13. **Technology:** Uses technology effectively to plan, teach, and assess.	

Comments:

Used with permission. Dr. Bill Kruskamp, former principal, Creekland Middle School, Gwinnett County Public Schools (Lawrenceville, GA).

Tool 5   Informal Classroom Observation: Essential Question and Answer Summarizing—Creekland Middle School

Angle: Narrow

Focus: Essential question and answer summarizing

Teacher: Date:

Essential questions (circle one):   Yes   No

- posted
- guided instruction
- used at the end of lessons to assist summarizing and gathering evidence of learning

Summarizing (circle one):   Yes   No

- reflects evidence of student learning
- all students participate
- guided by the essential question

What were the students doing?

Comments:

Used with permission. Dr. Bill Kruskamp, former principal, Creekland Middle School, Gwinnett County Public Schools (Lawrenceville, GA).

Tool 6   Selective Verbatim: Praise, Correction, and Preventive Prompts

Angle: Narrow

Focus: Teacher's skills in giving praise, correction, and preventive prompts

Teacher: Observer:

Date of Observation: Start Time: End Time:

Total Observation Time: Period of the Day:

Number of Students Present: Grade Level:

Class: Topic of the Lesson:

Date of Postobservation Conference:

Teacher Comment/Response	Time	Praise	Correction	Preventive Prompt
Ratio of praise to correction:		Preventive prompts:		

Developed by Theresa L. Benfante, Behavior Interventionist at Central Alternative School, Cobb County School District (Georgia). Used with permission.

Tool 7   Global Scan: Scripting Data by Time

Angle: Wide

Focus: General focus—everything that occurs in the classroom; events are recorded by time

Teacher: Observer:

Date of Observation: Start Time: End Time:

Total Observation Time: Period of the Day:

Number of Students Present: Grade Level:

Class: Topic of the Lesson:

Date of Postobservation Conference:

Time	Events that Occurred	Notes

This tool was developed by Oksana Parylo, a doctoral student at the University of Georgia, Athens. Used with permission.

Tool 8   Open-Ended Classroom Observation Form

Angle: Wide

Focus: General focus—everything that occurs in the classroom

Teacher: Observer:

Date of Observation: Start Time: End Time:

Total Observation Time: Period of the Day:

Number of Students Present: Grade Level:

Class: Location:

Objectives to Be Observed (If none specified, write, "general."):

Times	Observations
	Additional Observations

Tool 9   Open-Ended—Key Areas

Angle: Wide

Focus: Selected key areas (e.g., learning objectives, instructional strategies, seating arrangement, and calling patterns)

Teacher: Observer:

Date of Observation: Start Time: End Time:

Total Observation Time: Period of the Day:

Number of Students Present: Grade Level:

Class: Topic of the Lesson:

Date of Postobservation Conference:

I. Learning Objective:

II. Instructional Strategies (also note time):

III. Seating Arrangement:

IV. Transition Strategies:

V. Calling Patterns:

VI. Markers of Student Engagement:

Tool 10   Sample Checklist Classroom Observation Form

Angle: Narrow

Focus: Teacher's actions and/or students' actions

Teacher: Observer:

Date of Observation: Start Time: End Time:

Total Observation Time: Period of the Day:

Number of Students Present: Grade Level:

Class: Topic of the Lesson:

Date of Postobservation Conference:

Students were:

☐ working in small, cooperative groups

☐ making a presentation

☐ taking a test

☐ working independently at their desks

☐ viewing a film

☐ other _____

Teacher was:

☐ lecturing

☐ facilitating a question-and-answer sequence

☐ working independently with students

☐ demonstrating a concept

☐ introducing a new concept

☐ reviewing for a test

☐ coming to closure

☐ other _____

Comments:

Tool 11   Extended Checklist Classroom Observation Form

Angle: Narrow

Focus: Teacher's actions and/or students' actions

Teacher: Observer:

Date of Observation: Start Time: End Time:

Total Observation Time: Period of the Day:

Number of Students Present: Grade Level:

Class: Topic of the Lesson:

Date of Postobservation Conference:

Check	Students were...	Time	Notes
	Working in small, cooperative groups		
	Making a presentation		
	Taking a test		
	Working independently at their desks		
	Viewing a film		
	Other:		

Tool 12 Mixed-Method Informal Classroom Observations—Daves Creek Elementary School

Angle: Narrow

Focus: Learning environment (based on clearly defined criteria)

Teacher: Administrator:

Date of Observation: Time:

Learning Environment

Presence = X	Criteria	Example Evidence
	The classroom is neat/well organized; safety information is posted; Gotta Go Bag is accessible.	
	Artifacts are standards/curriculum-based, level appropriate, and incorporate student work.	
	Essential questions relating to lesson posted in an area for students to see.	
	Classroom rules clearly posted with rewards/consequences.	
	Transitions are appropriate and smooth.	
	Routines and procedures are in place and followed.	
	Students show engagement to current lesson or task.	
	Mutual respect is evident.	

This tool was developed by Eric Ashton, principal, and Peggy Baggett, assistant principal, of Daves Creek Elementary School, and Kathy Carpenter, now principal at Riverwatch Middle School, in Forsyth County Public Schools (GA). Used with permission.

Continued

Tool 12   Cont'd

Lesson Design and Delivery Incorporates the WOW* Design Qualities and Differentiation

Presence = X	Criteria	Example Evidence
	Varied strategies and use of graphic organizers are used to meet needs of diverse learners— ESOL, EIP, special ed, and gifted.	
	Student work is meaningful and has "real-life" application.	
	Students are provided with specific and descriptive feedback throughout lesson to target areas of improvement.	
	Varied levels of student work samples are posted for the purpose of student self-assessing against standards.	
	Support for reading and math AIM goals is evident.	
	Guided Reading Lessons: • Small-group reading purpose before and after • Running reading records • Genre • Graphic organizers • Questions/critical thinking	
	Variety of student grouping is used to meet individual student needs.	

Comments:

---

*WOW is "Working on the Work," a reform construct developed by Phil Schlechty (*Shaking Up the Schoolhouse*, 2000).

Tool 13   Literacy Classroom Observation Checklist

Angle: Narrow

Focus: Literacy block; guided reading; literacy strategies

Teacher: Observer:

Date of Observation: Start Time: End Time:

Total Observation Time: Number of Students Present:

Grade Level: Topic of the Lesson:

Date of Postobservation Conference:

Literacy Block	Guided Reading	Well Organized Classroom
☐ read aloud	☐ small group area evident	☐ posts and uses rules, schedules, management system
☐ phonemic awareness (K-2)	☐ uses appropriate narrative texts	☐ students routinely follow established rules and procedures
☐ concepts of print (K-2)	☐ uses appropriate informational texts	
☐ shared reading	☐ differentiates instruction to meet all students' needs	☐ smooth transitions
☐ guided reading	☐ uses before, during, after activities	☐ room organized, labeled
☐ centers/independent work	☐ incorporates comprehension	☐ seating arranged for cooperative learning activities and interaction
☐ Monitored Independent Reading (MIR)	☐ incorporates fluency	☐ students accountable for learning
☐ explicit whole-class instruction	☐ teaches vocabulary of text	
☐ word work	☐ listens to students read	☐ room clutter free, inviting
☐ phonics/spelling	☐ conducts running records	☐ productive, workable noise level
☐ comprehension	☐ has up-to-date records	
☐ fluency	☐ uses appropriate reading strategies (whisper, staggered, choral, paired, etc.) NO ROUND-ROBIN reading!	☐ teacher has positive interaction with students
☐ oral language		☐ positive interaction between students
☐ interactive/shared writing		
☐ modeled writing		
☐ directed writing		
☐ 6+1 traits of writing		
☐ writer's workshop		
☐ independent writing		

Continued

Tool 13   Cont'd

Literacy Rich Classroom	Centers/Independent Work	Explicit Instruction
☐ print-rich environment ☐ concept charts ☐ definition charts ☐ 6+1 Traits posters ☐ comprehension posters ☐ authentic reading/writing observed ☐ student writing displayed ☐ classroom library evident, with narrative & informational texts in a wide variety of genres, leveled appropriately, for student use ☐ leveled book boxes for MIR ☐ Word Wall posted, consisting of general and content words	☐ management system in place ☐ Students responsible for learning ☐ engaging activities ☐ authentic reading/writing activities ☐ student accountability system ☐ differentiated work matches student needs ☐ work reinforces previously taught concepts	☐ grade-level teacher talk ☐ shared reading—all students ☐ uses Houghton Mifflin for shared reading ☐ other grade-level texts (big books, poetry, informational); all students have access to text ☐ book talk ☐ preteaches vocabulary ☐ uses comprehension strategies before, during, after activities ☐ interactive, hands-on activities ☐ integrated content core ☐ incorporates good ESL strategies
Writing	MIR	Word Work
☐ writing process ☐ mini lesson ☐ 6+1 traits of writing ☐ student accountability/status of class ☐ interactive/shared writing (K-2) ☐ modeled writing ☐ directed writing ☐ independent writing ☐ student published writing available to other students ☐ writing area & materials evident	☐ minimum 15–20 minutes per day ☐ students self-select books from independent reading level; interest based books provided by teacher ☐ variety of genres provided ☐ monitoring, nongraded (student reflections, cooperative learning discussions, conferences, bookmarks, journals, pictures, etc.)	☐ phonemic awareness (K-2) ☐ phonics ☐ vocabulary ☐ differentiated spelling ☐ grade-level Language Arts ☐ Word Wall posted ☐ Word Wall systematically used in instruction
Assessment	Collaboration	Curriculum Mapping
☐ keeps up-to-date running records with guided reading levels ☐ submits guided reading levels as requested ☐ maintains detailed formal and informal assessment records ☐ maintains list of below level students	☐ collaborates with team in analyzing assessment data ☐ collaboratively plans for/ provides interventions, reteaching, enrichment, differentiation	☐ creates curriculum map based on Utah State Core and student needs ☐ uses curriculum map to guide instruction

This tool was developed by the Jordan School District, Sandy, UT. Acknowledgement is given to Dana L. Bickmore, former executive director for curriculum and staff development, and Kathy Ridd, elementary language arts and early childhood consultant of the Jordan School District. Used with permission.

Tool 14 Anecdotal and Checklist Data-Collection Method: Focus on Cooperative Learning

Angle: Narrow

Focus: One or more aspects of cooperative learning (e.g., objectives, clarity of directions, and follow-up instructions)

Teacher: Observer:

Date of Observation: Start Time: End Time:

Total Observation Time: Period of the Day:

Number of Students Present: Grade Level:

Class: Topic of the Lesson:

Date of Postobservation Conference:

Focus	Presence = X	Notes
Objectives for the cooperative learning group		
Clarity of directions		
Movement into groups		
Monitoring and intervening strategies		
Interaction with students		
Follow-up instruction		

Tool 15 Foreign Language Observation Checklist

Angle: Narrow

Focus: One or more aspects of foreign language teaching and learning (e.g., language modalities, culture, and learning materials)

Teacher: Observer:

Date of Observation: Start Time: End Time:

Total Observation Time: Period of the Day:

Number of Students Present: Grade Level:

Class: Topic of the Lesson:

Date of Postobservation Conference:

1. Are all language modalities evident in the lesson (speaking, writing, listening, and reading)?

2. Is culture evident in the lesson?

3. Does the teacher use a wide variety of prepared and authentic materials at appropriate levels?

4. Is the purpose of each activity clearly explained to the students?

5. Does the teacher model activities when giving directions and check for comprehension afterward?

6. Are the transitions between activities smooth?

7. Are the students on task and actively involved in the learning process?

8. Is there an appropriate use of partner–pair or small group activities?

Developed by Marcia Wilbur, Ph.D., executive director, Curriculum and Content Development for the Advanced Placement Programs at the College Board, based on her work at Gull Lake High School Department, Richland, Michigan. Used with permission.

Tool 16   Sample Seating Chart

Angle: Narrow

Focus: Events; teacher questions; student responses

Teacher: Observer:

Date of Observation: Start Time: End Time:

Total Observation Time: Period of the Day:

Number of Students Present: Grade Level:

Class: Topic of the Lesson:

Date of Postobservation Conference:

Tool 17   Extended Seating Chart

Angle: Narrow

Focus: One or more aspects of classroom activities (e.g., questions, culture, and learning materials)

Teacher: Observer:

Date of Observation: Start Time: End Time:

Total Observation Time: Period of the Day:

Number of Students Present: Grade Level:

Class: Topic of the Lesson:

Observation Foci:

Observation Legend:

This tool was developed by Oksana Parylo, a doctoral student at the University of Georgia, Athens. Used with permission.

Tool 18   Observation Guide Using Bloom's Taxonomy

Angle: Narrow

Focus: Questioning strategies based on the class discussion

Teacher: Observer:

Date of Observation: Start Time: End Time:

Total Observation Time: Period of the Day:

Number of Students Present: Grade Level:

Class: Topic of the Lesson:

Date of Postobservation Conference:

Time	Questions and Activities	Levels of Thinking					
		Knowledge	Comprehension	Application	Analysis	Synthesis	Evaluation

Tool 19   Alternative Observation Guide Using Bloom's Taxonomy

Angle: Narrow

Focus: Questioning strategies based on the class discussion

Teacher: Observer:

Date of Observation: Start Time: End Time:

Total Observation Time: Period of the Day:

Number of Students Present: Grade Level:

Class: Topic of the Lesson:

Date of Postobservation Conference:

Time	Teacher Questions	Taxonomy Level

Tool 20 Using Bloom's Taxonomy to Analyze Student Questions

Angle: Narrow

Focus: Student questions

Teacher: Observer:

Date of Observation: Start Time: End Time:

Total Observation Time: Period of the Day:

Number of Students Present: Grade Level:

Class: Topic of the Lesson:

Date of Postobservation Conference:

Time	Student Questions	Taxonomy Level

Tool 21 Extended Observation Guide Using Bloom's Taxonomy

Angle: Narrow

Focus: One or more aspects of classroom focusing on teacher questions

Teacher: Observer:

Date of Observation: Start Time: End Time:

Total Observation Time: Period of the Day:

Number of Students Present: Grade Level:

Class: Topic of the Lesson:

Date of Postobservation Conference:

Time	Teacher Questions	Directed to: Class (C) Individual (I)	Taxonomy Level

This tool was developed by Oksana Parylo, a doctoral student at the University of Georgia, Athens. Used with permission.

Tool 22   Focus on Wait Time

Angle: Narrow

Focus: Wait time during class discussion or lecture

Teacher: Observer:

Date of Observation: Start Time: End Time:

Total Observation Time: Period of the Day:

Number of Students Present: Grade Level:

Class: Topic of the Lesson:

Date of Postobservation Conference:

Teacher Questions	Wait Time (Seconds)

Tool 23   Using Bloom's Taxonomy to Examine Levels of Questions

Angle: Narrow

Focus: Examining teacher questions and/or student questions

Teacher: Observer:

Date of Observation: Start Time: End Time:

Total Observation Time: Period of the Day:

Number of Students Present: Grade Level:

Class: Topic of the Lesson:

Date of Postobservation Conference:

Teacher Questions	Wait Time (Seconds)	Question Domain

Tool 24   Using Bloom's Taxonomy to Examine Levels of Questions
(Extended)

Angle: Narrow

Focus: Examining teacher questions and/or student questions

Teacher: Observer:

Date of Observation: Start Time: End Time:

Total Observation Time: Period of the Day:

Number of Students Present: Grade Level:

Class: Topic of the Lesson:

Date of Postobservation Conference:

Teacher Questions	Directed to: Class (C) Male Student (M) Female Student (F)	Wait Time (Seconds)	Taxonomy Level

This tool was developed by Oksana Parylo, a doctoral student at the University of Georgia, Athens. Used with permission.

Tool 25   Tracking Calling Patterns

Angle: Narrow

Focus: Calling and interaction patterns during a class period

Teacher: Observer:

Date of Observation: Start Time: End Time:

Total Observation Time: Period of the Day:

Number of Students Present: Grade Level:

Class: Topic of the Lesson:

Date of Postobservation Conference:

Legend

Entire Class Response: ECR   Individual Response: IR

Individual Help: IH   Question: Q   Comment: C

Front of Room

	A	B	C	D
1				
2				
3				
4				
5				

Tool 26 Tracking Calling Patterns—Seating Chart

Angle: Narrow

Focus: Calling and interaction patterns during a class period

The following approach focuses broadly on the distribution of calling patterns across boys and girls.

Teacher: Observer:

Date of Observation: Start Time: End Time:

Total Observation Time: Period of the Day:

Number of Students Present: Grade Level:

Class: Topic of the Lesson:

Date of Postobservation Conference:

This tool was developed by Meredith A. Byrd, Clayton County Public Schools (Jonesboro, GA). Used with permission.

Tool 27   Cause and Effect

Angle: Narrow

Focus: Tracking teacher behaviors to determine the effects they have on students

Teacher: Observer:

Date of Observation: Start Time: End Time:

Total Observation Time: Period of the Day:

Number of Students Present: Grade Level:

Class: Topic of the Lesson:

Date of Postobservation Conference:

Time	Teacher	Student Response or Activity

156

Tool 28 Alternative Approach to Cause and Effect

Angle: Narrow

Focus: Tracking teacher behaviors to determine the effects they have on students

Teacher: Observer:

Date of Observation: Start Time: End Time:

Total Observation Time: Period of the Day:

Number of Students Present: Grade Level:

Class: Topic of the Lesson:

Date of Postobservation Conference:

Time	Student Behavior		Teacher Response
	Individual Students	**Students as a Class**	

This tool was developed by Oksana Parylo, a doctoral student at the University of Georgia, Athens. Used with permission.

Tool 29   Variety of Instructional Methods

Angle: Narrow

Focus: Instructional techniques; instructional materials used by the teacher

Teacher: Observer:

Date of Observation: Start Time: End Time:

Total Observation Time: Period of the Day:

Number of Students Present: Grade Level:

Class: Topic of the Lesson:

Date of Postobservation Conference:

Time	Instructional Method	Teacher Behavior	Student Activities

Tool 30 Examining Teacher-Student Discussion with a Focus on How Student Comments Are Incorporated into the Lesson

Angle: Narrow

Focus: Incorporating student comments and ideas into the discussion

Teacher: Observer:

Date of Observation: Start Time: End Time:

Total Observation Time: Period of the Day:

Number of Students Present: Grade Level:

Class: Topic of the Lesson:

Date of Postobservation Conference:

Time	Teacher Talk/Question	Student Responses	How Student Comments Are Used

159

Tool 31 Focus on Tracking Transition Patterns

Angle: Narrow

Focus: Transition strategies during instruction and classroom activities

Teacher: Observer:

Date of Observation: Start Time: End Time:

Total Observation Time: Period of the Day:

Number of Students Present: Grade Level:

Class: Topic of the Lesson:

Date of Postobservation Conference:

Instruction/Activity	Transition	Student Response

160

Tool 32   Tracking Student Behavior

Angle: Narrow

Focus: Student behavior

Teacher: Observer:

Date of Observation: Start Time: End Time:

Total Observation Time: Period of the Day:

Number of Students Present: Grade Level:

Class: Topic of the Lesson:

Date of Postobservation Conference:

Time	Teacher	Student

161

Tool 33   Classroom Traffic—Seating Chart

Angle: Narrow

Focus: Teacher moving around the room and contacting students; teacher proximity

Teacher: Observer:

Date of Observation: Start Time: End Time:

Total Observation Time: Period of the Day:

Number of Students Present: Grade Level:

Class: Topic of the Lesson:

Date of Postobservation Conference:

Tool 34   Beginning of Class Routines

Angle: Narrow

Focus: Activities within the first 15 minutes of the class

Teacher: Observer:

Date of Observation: Start Time: End Time:

Total Observation Time: Period of the Day:

Number of Students Present: Grade Level:

Class: Topic of the Lesson:

Date of Postobservation Conference:

Time	Beginning of the Period	Student Behavior

Tool 35   Tracking End of Class Routines

Angle: Narrow

Focus: Activities within the last 15 minutes of the class

Teacher: Observer:

Date of Observation: Start Time: End Time:

Total Observation Time: Period of the Day:

Number of Students Present: Grade Level:

Class: Topic of the Lesson:

Date of Postobservation Conference:

Time	Ending of the Period	Student Behavior

Tool 36   Focus on Cooperative Learning

Angle: Narrow

Focus: Student interaction and teacher monitoring

Teacher: Observer:

Date of Observation: Start Time: End Time:

Total Observation Time: Period of the Day:

Number of Students Present: Grade Level:

Class: Topic of the Lesson:

Date of Postobservation Conference:

Focus	Notes

Tool 37   Cooperative Learning—Student Interactions and Teacher Monitoring

Angle: Narrow

Focus: Student interaction and teacher monitoring

Teacher: Observer:

Date of Observation: Start Time: End Time:

Total Observation Time: Period of the Day:

Number of Students Present: Grade Level:

Class: Topic of the Lesson:

Date of Postobservation Conference:

Group	Number in Group	Student Interaction	Teacher Monitoring Strategies

Tool 38 Tracking Teacher Behaviors Promoting Cooperative Learning

Angle: Narrow

Focus: Teacher behavior; cooperative learning

Teacher: Observer:

Date of Observation: Start Time: End Time:

Total Observation Time: Period of the Day:

Number of Students Present: Grade Level:

Class: Topic of the Lesson:

Date of Postobservation Conference:

Focus on Cooperative Learning	Presence or Absence	Notes
Objectives for the cooperative learning group		
Clarity of directions		
Movement into groups		
Monitoring and intervening strategies		
Evaluation Strategies		
Interaction with students		
Follow-up instruction—large-group processing		

Tool 39   Classroom Observation Guide to Track Technology Integration

Angle: Narrow

Focus: How technology is integrated within teaching

Teacher: Observer:

Date of Observation: Start Time: End Time:

Total Observation Time: Period of the Day:

Number of Students Present: Grade Level:

Class: Topic of the Lesson:

Date of Postobservation Conference:

Indicators for Technology Integration

Rate each of the following using this rating scale:

    1 = Little evidence of technology use

    2 = Some evidence that technology is used in limited amounts and with simple tasks—more productivity oriented

    3 = Evidence that teacher uses technology and provides assistance to students with spreadsheets, word processing, demonstrations

    4 = Teacher is comfortable with technology use; a variety of technology is used daily, and technology is an integral part of classroom instruction

    5 = Not applicable to the lesson

___ 1. Students use computers for drill and practice activities; use of stand-alone computer software.
- Use of networkable programs, such as Accelerated Reader and Accelerated Math
- Use of instructional Web-based software, such as Riverdeep

___ 2. Students use computers for instructional purposes.
- Use of computers for performance assessments, such as PowerPoint and Excel
- Use of computers for Web-based research using computers to gather data
- Use of a combination of software and Web-based research to analyze data and draw conclusions
- Taking data and conclusions and presenting it using some type of multimedia presentation

___ 3. Teacher uses presentation software, such as PowerPoint during instruction.

___ 4. Teacher uses projection tools during instruction.
- Uses overhead projector
- Uses multimedia projector
- Uses multimedia projector with VCR
- Uses multimedia projector with SmartBoard or ActivBoard

Continued

___ 5. Teacher incorporates the use of other devices during instruction.
  • Digital camera
  • Scanner
  • iPod
  • Graphing calculators

___ 6. Teacher incorporates technology within the lesson, and student work is indicative of seamless transitions between traditional instruction and technology integration.

Classroom Observation Running Notes

The Classroom Observation Guide to Track Technology Integration Tool was developed by Ann G. Haughey, as part of her coursework in supervision theory, and her problem of practice, while working toward her specialist in education degree at the University of Georgia. Ann G. Haughey is the technology coordinator for Wilkes County Schools (Washington, GA). Used with permission.

Tool 40   Running Notes with a Timeline

Angle: Wide

Focus: Open-ended; no focus

Teacher: Observer:

Date of Observation: Start Time: End Time:

Total Observation Time: Period of the Day:

Number of Students Present: Grade Level:

Class: Topic of the Lesson:

Date of Postobservation Conference:

Time	Running Notes

Tool 41   Alternative Approach to Running Notes with a Timeline

Angle: Wide

Focus: Open-ended; no focus

Teacher: Observer:

Date of Observation: Start Time: End Time:

Total Observation Time: Period of the Day:

Number of Students Present: Grade Level:

Class: Topic of the Lesson:

Date of Postobservation Conference:

Time	Teacher	Students	Other

Tool 42 Evidence of Interdisciplinary Teaching with a Focus on Teacher's Comments and Questions and Student Responses

Angle: Narrow

Focus: Teacher's comments and questions and student responses

Teacher: Observer:

Date of Observation: Start Time: End Time:

Total Observation Time: Period of the Day:

Number of Students Present: Grade Level:

Class: Topic of the Lesson:

Date of Postobservation Conference:

Note: C/Q=comments/questions; SR=student response; T=time

Math	Science	Social Studies	Language Arts	Connections
T: C/Q: T: SR:	T: C/Q: T: SR:	T: C/Q: T: SR:	T: C/Q: T: SR:	T: C/Q: T: SR:
T: C/Q: T: SR:	T: C/Q: T: SR:	T: C/Q: T: SR:	T: C/Q: T: SR:	T: C/Q: T: SR:

Tool 43   Evidence of Interdisciplinary Teaching with a Focus on Students' Comments and Questions and Teacher Responses

Angle: Narrow

Focus: Students' comments and questions and teacher responses

Teacher: Observer:

Date of Observation: Start Time: End Time:

Total Observation Time: Period of the Day:

Number of Students Present: Grade Level:

Class: Topic of the Lesson:

Date of Postobservation Conference:

Note: C/Q=comments/questions; TR=teacher response; T=time

Math	Science	Social Studies	Language Arts	Connections
T: C/Q:	T: C/Q:	T: C/Q:	T: C/Q:	T: C/Q:
T: TR:	T: TR:	T: TR:	T: TR:	T: TR:
T: C/Q:	T: C/Q: T	T: C/Q:	T: C/Q:	T: C/Q:
T: TR:	T: TR:	T: TR:	T: TR:	T: TR:

Developed by Angela Kanellopoulos and Lauren Moret. Used with permission.

Tool 44 Sample Informal Postobservation Feedback Form

Purpose: A form to assist the observer during the postobservation

Teacher: Observer:

Date of Observation: Start Time: End Time:

Total Observation Time: Period of the Day:

Number of Students Present: Grade Level:

Class: Topic of the Lesson:

Date of Postobservation Conference:

Students were:

☐ working in small, cooperative groups

☐ making a presentation

☐ taking a test

☐ working independently at their desks

☐ viewing a film

☐ other:

Teacher was:

☐ lecturing

☐ facilitating a question and answer sequence

☐ working independently with students

☐ demonstrating a concept

☐ introducing a new concept

☐ reviewing for a test

☐ coming to closure

☐ other

Comments:

Tool 45   Alternative Informal Postobservation Feedback Form

Purpose: Alternative form to assist the observer during the postobservation

Teacher: Observer:

Date of Observation: Start Time: End Time:

Total Observation Time: Period of the Day:

Number of Students Present: Grade Level:

Class: Topic of the Lesson:

Observation Focus: Observation Tool Used:

Place of Postobservation Conference:

Date of Postobservation Conference:

Instruction

- Learning objectives: What will the students learn?

- What did instruction look and sound like? What did the teacher do and what did the students do?

- What instructional strategies were used?

- What resources and materials did the teacher use throughout the lesson?

Data Analysis

- What can we conclude from observational data?

- What can be done to improve instruction in the future?

Feedback

Tool 46   Presentation of Postobservation Conference Notes

Purpose: Organization of observation notes for the postobservation conference

Teacher: Observer:

Date of Observation: Start Time: End Time:

Total Observation Time: Period of the Day:

Number of Students Present: Grade Level:

Class: Topic of the Lesson:

Date of Postobservation Conference:

Time	Running Notes	Teacher Questions

Tool 47   Tracking Sheet—Faculty Needs

Purpose: Tracking the needs of the faculty

Teacher: Years:

Years at School:

Short-Term Instructional Goal(s):

Long-Term Instructional Goal(s):

Log of Informal Observations

Observation Date:

Follow-Up:

Observation Date:

Follow-Up:

Observation Date:

Follow-Up:

Observation Date:

Follow-Up:

Tool 48   Questions to Lead the Teacher Talk about Student-Generated Artifacts

Purpose: A guide for examining student-generated artifacts

1. What information about student learning have you gleaned from the student thoughts and proofs from the cards?

2. Do students use the cards later to write essays?

3. Today, what will you do to review the proofs and the cards with students?

4. What do these artifacts tell you about what you are teaching and why?

5. If you could rework the lesson from yesterday, what would you do differently and why?

6. How can this lesson and in-class assignment be modified based on the patterns found in these cards and the proofs?

Tool 49   Thinking, Listening, and Reflecting with Colleagues
about Student Work

Purpose: A protocol to be used in postobservation conference to examine student work

---

Reflecting on the Process

Looking for evidence of student thinking...

- What did you see in this student's work that was interesting or surprising?
- What did you learn about how this student thinks and learns?
- What about the process helped you see and learn these things?

Reflecting on one's own thinking...

- What questions about teaching and assessment did looking at the students' work raise for you?
- How can you pursue these questions further?
- Are there things you would like to try in your classroom as a result of looking at this student's work?

Tool 50   Examining Student Work by Content Standards

Purpose: Examining student work around content standards

Teacher: Observer:

Date of Observation: Start Time: End Time:

Total Observation Time: Period of the Day:

Number of Students Present: Grade Level:

Class: Topic of the Lesson:

Date of Postobservation Conference:

Artifact:

Narrative Analysis of Grade-Level-Appropriate Text

Writing Strategies

Organization and Focus

Research and Technology

Questions to Guide the Examination and Discussion:

Tool 51 Planning Guide—What Next?

Purpose: Prompts to help principals talk about instruction planning

1. What content needs to be reviewed or retaught based on the discussion during the postobservation conference?

2. What instructional strategies would most likely help move learning forward to meet goals and objectives?

3. What materials are needed?

Tool Index

Tool #	Tool Name	Angle	Focus/Purpose	Page #
1	Assessing the Broad Characteristics of a Faculty	N/A	Broadly assess the characteristics of a faculty	6
2	Assessing Individual Teachers	N/A	Broadly assess individual teachers	9
3	Tracking Informal Observations	N/A	Keep a record of the conducted informal classroom observations	13
4	Focused Informal Classroom Observations—Creekland Middle School	Narrow	Instructional strategies; classroom expectations	21
5	Informal Classroom Observation: Essential Question and Answer Summarizing—Creekland Middle School	Narrow	Essential questions; summarizing	22
6	Selective Verbatim: Praise, Correction, and Preventive Prompts	Narrow	Teacher's skills in giving praise, correction, and preventive prompts	31
7	Global Scan: Scripting Data by Time	Wide	General focus: everything that occurs in the classroom; events are recorded by time	32
8	Open-Ended Classroom Observation Form	Wide	General focus: everything that occurs in the classroom	34
9	Open-Ended—Key Areas	Wide	Selected key areas (e.g., learning objectives, instructional strategies, seating arrangement, and calling patterns)	35
10	Sample Checklist Classroom Observation Form	Narrow	Teacher's actions and/or students' actions	36
11	Extended Checklist Classroom Observation Form	Narrow	Teacher's actions and/or students' actions	37

Tool #	Tool Name	Angle	Focus/Purpose	Page #
12	Mixed-Method Informal Classroom Observations—Daves Creek Elementary School	Narrow	Learning environment (based on clearly defined criteria)	38
13	Literacy Classroom Observation Checklist	Narrow	Literacy block; guided reading; literacy strategies	40
14	Anecdotal and Checklist Data-Collection Method: Focus on Cooperative Learning	Narrow	One or more aspects of cooperative learning (e.g., objectives, clarity of directions, and follow-up instructions)	42
15	Foreign Language Observation Checklist	Narrow	One or more aspects of foreign language teaching and learning (e.g., language modalities, culture, and learning materials)	43
16	Sample Seating Chart	Narrow	Events; teacher questions; student responses	44
17	Extended Seating Chart	Narrow	One or more aspects of classroom activities (e.g., questions, culture, and learning materials)	46
18	Observation Guide Using Bloom's Taxonomy	Narrow	Questioning strategies based on the class discussion	54
19	Alternative Observation Guide Using Bloom's Taxonomy	Narrow	Questioning strategies based on the class discussion	56
20	Using Bloom's Taxonomy to Analyze Student Questions	Narrow	Student questions	57
21	Extended Observation Guide Using Bloom's Taxonomy	Narrow	One or more aspects of classroom focusing on teacher questions	58
22	Focus on Wait Time	Narrow	Wait time during class discussion or lecture	59
23	Using Bloom's Taxonomy to Examine Levels of Questions	Narrow	Examining teacher questions and/or student questions	61
24	Using Bloom's Taxonomy to Examine Levels of Questions (Extended)	Narrow	Examining teacher questions and/or student questions	62
25	Tracking Calling Patterns	Narrow	Calling and interaction patterns during a class period	64
26	Tracking Calling Patterns—Seating Chart	Narrow	Calling and interaction patterns during a class period	65
27	Cause and Effect	Narrow	Tracking teacher behaviors to determine the effects they have on students	67

Tool #	Tool Name	Angle	Focus/Purpose	Page #
28	Alternative Approach to Cause and Effect	Narrow	Tracking teacher behaviors to determine the effects they have on students	68
29	Variety of Instructional Methods	Narrow	Instructional techniques; instructional methods used by the teacher	71
30	Examining Teacher-Student Discussion with a Focus on How Student Comments Are Incorporated into the Lesson	Narrow	Incorporating student comments and ideas into the discussion	73
31	Focus on Tracking Transition Patterns	Narrow	Transition strategies during instruction and classroom activities	75
32	Tracking Student Behavior	Narrow	Student behavior	77
33	Classroom Traffic—Seating Chart	Narrow	Teacher moving around the room and contacting students; teacher proximity	80
34	Beginning of Class Routines	Narrow	Activities within the first 15 minutes of the class	82
35	Tracking End of Class Routines	Narrow	Activities within the last 15 minutes of the class	84
36	Focus on Cooperative Learning	Narrow	Students' work in the cooperative groups	87
37	Cooperative Learning—Student Interactions and Teacher Monitoring	Narrow	Student interaction and teacher monitoring	89
38	Tracking Teacher Behaviors Promoting Cooperative Learning	Narrow	Teacher behavior; cooperative learning	90
39	Classroom Observation Guide to Track Technology Integration	Narrow	How technology is integrated within teaching	93
40	Running Notes with a Timeline	Wide	Open-ended; no focus	96
41	Alternative Approach to Running Notes with a Timeline	Wide	Open-ended; no focus	97
42	Evidence of Interdisciplinary Teaching with a Focus on Teacher's Comments and Questions and Student Responses	Narrow	Teacher's comments and questions and student responses	100
43	Evidence of Interdisciplinary Teaching with a Focus on Students' Comments and Questions and Teacher Responses	Narrow	Students' comments and questions and student responses	102

Tool #	Tool Name	Angle	Focus/Purpose	Page #
44	Sample Informal Postobservation Feedback Form	N/A	A form to assist the principal during the postobservation	106
45	Alternative Informal Postobservation Feedback Form	N/A	Alternative form to assist the principal during the postobservation	107
46	Presentation of Postobservation Conference Notes	N/A	Organization of observation notes for the postobservation conference	109
47	Tracking Sheet—Faculty Needs	N/A	Tracking the needs of the faculty	116
48	Questions to Lead the Teacher Talk about Student-Generated Artifacts	N/A	A guide for examining student-generated artifacts	121
49	Thinking, Listening, and Reflecting with Colleagues about Student Work	N/A	A protocol to be used in postobservation conference to examine student work	122
50	Examining Student Work by Content Standards	N/A	Examining student work around content standards	123
51	Planning Guide—What Next?	N/A	Prompts to help principals talk about instruction planning	124

References

Abrami, P. C., Bernard, R. M., Borokhovski, E., Wade, A., Surkes, M. A., & Zhang, D. (2008). Instructional interventions affecting critical thinking skills and dispositions: A stage 1 meta-analysis. *Review of Educational Research, 78*(4), 1102–1134. doi:10.3102/0034654308326084

Acheson, K. A., & Gall, M. D. (1997). *Techniques in the clinical supervision of teachers: Preservice and inservice applications* (4th ed.). White Plains, NY: Longman.

ATLAS Learning Communities, Inc. (2007). ATLAS—*Learning from student work*. Cambridge, MA: ATLAS Learning Communities, Inc.

Barton, K., & Smith, L. (2000). Themes or motifs? Aiming for coherence through interdisciplinary outlines. *Reading Teacher, 54*(1), 54–63. Retrieved from http://web.ebsohost.com/

Bellon, J. J., & Bellon, E. C. (1982). *Classroom supervision and instructional improvement: A synergetic process* (2nd ed.). Dubuque, IA: Kendall/Hunt.

Bernhardt, V. (2007). *Translating data into information to improve teaching and learning*. Larchmont, NY: Eye On Education.

Blase, J. R., & Blase, J. J. (1998). *Handbook of instructional leadership: How really good principals promote teaching and learning*. Thousand Oaks, CA: Corwin Press.

Bloom, B. S. (Ed.). (1956). *Taxonomy of educational objectives: The classification of educational goals*. New York, NY: Longman.

Brookfield, S. D. (1986). *Understanding and facilitating adult learning: A comprehensive analysis of principles and effective practices*. San Francisco, CA: Jossey-Bass.

Burden, P. (1982, February). *Developmental supervision: Reducing teacher stress at different career stages*. Paper presented at the Association of Teacher Educators National Conference, Phoenix, AZ.

Burke, P. J., Christensen, J. C., & Fessler, R. (1984). *Teacher career stages: Implications for staff development*. Bloomington, IN: Phi Delta Kappa Educational Foundation.

Center for Comprehensive School Reform and Improvement. (2007). *Using the classroom walk-through as an instructional leadership strategy*. Washington, DC: Learning Point Associates.

Christensen, J. P., Burke, P. J., Fessler, R., & Hagstrom, D. (1983). *Stages of teachers' careers: Implications for professional development*. Washington, DC: National Institute of Education. (ERIC Document Reproduction Service No. ED227054).

Clark, K. (2010). Helping the environment helps the human race: Differentiated instruction across the curriculum. *Science Scope, 33*(6), 36–41.

Coffey, H. (2010). *Interdisciplinary teaching [UNC School of Education]*. Retrieved from http://www.learnnc.org/lp/pages/5196

Collins, A., Brown, J., & Newman, S. (1989). Cognitive apprenticeship: Teaching the crafts of reading, writing, and mathematics. In L. Resnick (Ed.), *Knowing, learning, and instruction: Essays in honor of Robert Glaser* (pp. 453–494). Hillsdale, NJP: Lawrence Erlbaum Associates, Inc.

Danielson, C. (2007). *Enhancing professional practice: A framework for teaching* (2nd ed.). Alexandria, VA: Association for Supervision and Curriculum Development.

Downey, C. J., Steffy, B. E., English, F. W., Frase, L. E., & Poston, W. K., Jr. (2004). *Changing school supervisory practices one teacher at a time: The three-minute classroom walk-through.* Thousand Oaks, CA: Corwin.

Downey, C. J., Steffy, B. E., English, F. W., Frase, L. E., & Poston, W. K., Jr. (2009). *Advancing the three-minute walk-through: Mastering reflective practice.* Thousand Oaks, CA: Corwin.

Egan, T. M., Cobb, B., & Anastasia, M. (2009). Think time: Formative assessment empowers teachers to try new practices. *Journal of Staff Development, 30*(4), 40–42.

Feiman, S., & Floden, R. (1980). *What's all this talk about teacher development?* East Lansing, MI: Institute for Research on Teaching. (ERIC Document Reproduction Service No. ED189088).

Frodeman, R., Klein, J. T., & Mitcham, C. (Eds.). (2010). The Oxford handbook of interdisciplinarity. Oxford, UK: Oxford University Press.

FutureCents. (2005). *Twelve guidelines for managing by walking around (MBWA).* Retrieved from www.futurecents.com/mainmbwa.htm

Gall, M. D., & Acheson, K. A. (2011). *Clinical supervision and teacher development: Preservice and inservice applications* (6th ed.). Hoboken, NJ: John Wiley & Sons.

Huberman, M. (1993). *The lives of teachers* (J. Neufeld, Trans.). New York, NY: Teachers College Press.

Hunzicker, J. (2010). *Characteristics of effective professional development: A checklist.* Retrieved from http://www.eric.ed.gov/PDFS/ED510366.pdf

Jacobs, H. H. (1989). The growing need for interdisciplinary curriculum content. In H. H. Jacobs (Ed.), *Interdisciplinary curriculum: Design and implementation* (pp. 1–12). Alexandria, VA: Association for Supervision and Curriculum Development.

Johnson, D. W., & Johnson, R. T. (1994). Learning together. In S. Sharan (Ed.), *Handbook of cooperative learning methods* (pp. 51–65). Westport, CT: Greenwood Press.

Katz, L. (1972). Developmental stages of preschool teachers. *Elementary School Journal, 73*(1), 50–54.

Knowles, M. S. (1973). *The adult learner: A neglected species.* Houston, TX: Gulf Publishing Co.

Knowles, M. S. (1980). *The modern practice of adult education: From pedagogy to andragogy* (2nd ed.). Chicago, IL: Follett.

Knowles, M. S., Swanson, R. A., & Holton, E. F. (2011). *The adult learner: The definitive classic in adult education and human resource development* (7th ed.). Burlington, MA: Butterworth-Heinemann.

Kurtoglu-Hooton, N. (2004, July). Postobservation feedback as an instigator of teacher learning and change. *International Association of Teachers of English as a Foreign Language TTED SIG E-Newsletter.* Retrieved from www.ihes.com/ttsig/resources/e-newsletter/FreatureArticles.pdf

Manning, R. C. (1988). *The teacher evaluation handbook: Step-by-step techniques and forms for improving instruction.* Paramus, NJ: Prentice Hall.

McDonald, J. (2001). Students' work and teachers' learning. In A. Lieberman & L. Miller (Eds.), *Teachers caught in the action: Professional development that matters* (pp. 209–235). New York, NY: Teachers College Press.

McGreal, T. L. (1983). *Effective teacher evaluation*. Alexandria, VA: Association for Supervision and Curriculum Development.

McGreal, T. L. (1988). Evaluation for enhancing instruction: Linking teacher evaluation and staff development. In S. J. Stanley & W. J. Popham (Eds.), *Teacher evaluation: Six prescriptions for success* (pp. 1–29). Alexandria, VA: Association for Supervision and Curriculum Development.

National Education Association Foundation for the Improvement of Education. (2003). *Using data about classroom practice and student work to improve professional development for educators*. Washington, DC: National Education Association Foundation for the Improvement of Education.

Nevills, P. (2003). Cruising the cerebral superhighway. *Journal of Staff Development, 24*(1), 20–23.

Northwest Regional Educational Laboratory (NREL). (n.d.). *Overview of technology integration in schools*. Portland, OR: Northwest Regional Educational Laboratory. Retrieved from http://www.netc.org/images/pdf/tech.integration.pdf

Palandra, M. (2010). The role of instructional supervision in district-wide reform. *International Journal of Leadership in Education, 13*(2), 221–234. doi:10.1080/13603120903144459.

Peters, T. J., & Waterman, R. H., Jr. (1982). *In search of excellence: Lessons from America's best run companies*. New York, NY: Harper & Row.

Rowe, M. B. (1986). Wait time: Slowing down may be a way of speeding up. *Journal of Teacher Education, 37*(1), 43–50. doi: 10.117/0022487186037001100

Schlechty, P. (2000). *Shaking up the schoolhouse*. San Francisco, CA: Jossey-Bass.

Sparks, D., & Hirsh, S. (1997). *A new vision for staff development*. Oxford, OH: National Staff Development Council.

Stahl, R. J. (1994). *Using "think-time" and "wait-time" skillfully in the class-room*. Bloomington, IN: ERIC Clearinghouse for Social Studies/Social Science Education. Retrieved from http://atozteacherstuff.com/ pages/1884.shtml

Tobin, K. (1987). The role of wait time in higher cognitive level learning. *Review of Educational Research, 57*(1), 69–95. doi: 10.3102/00346543057001069

Tomlinson, C. A. (1999). *The differentiated classroom: Responding to the needs of all learners*. Alexandria, VA: Association for Supervision and Curriculum Development.

Wang, C. M., & Ong, G. (2003). *Questioning techniques for active learning. Ideas on teaching*. Retrieved from http://www.cdtl.nus.edu.sg/ideas/iot2.htm

Wood, F. H., & Killian, J. E. (1998). Job-embedded learning makes the difference in school improvement. *Journal of Staff Development, 19*(1), 52–54.

Zepeda, S. J. (2007a). *The principal as instructional leader: A handbook for supervisors* (2nd ed.). Larchmont, NY: Eye On Education.

Zepeda, S. J. (2007b). *Instructional supervision: Applying tools and concepts* (2nd ed.). Larchmont, NY: Eye On Education.

Zepeda, S. J. (2008). *Professional development: What works*. Larchmont, NY: Eye On Education.